A COLLECTION O

CATS

TALES

A Collection Of Cats' Tales

Paintings by Ditz

Published by AAPPL Artists' and Photographers' Press Ltd
10 Hillside London SW19 4NH UK
info@aappl.com   www.aappl.com

Sales and Distribution
UK and export: Turnaround Publisher Services sales@turnaround-uk.com
Australia and New Zealand: Peribo Pty peribomec@bigpond.com

ISBN 1-904332-30-7 ISBN 978-1-904332-30-5

Art Director: Ditz   info@aappl.com
Design: Stefan Nekuda office@nekuda.at

Printed in Singapore by Imago Publishing   info@imago.co.uk

Dedication

For my husband, without whom this book
could have been made in half the time…

And Thanks…

Thanks to my parents who lovingly nurtured my imagination and encouraged me to paint, to my husband, without whom this book would not actually have been possible, to my daughter, Julie, who sat for me when she was little and who also appears in this book, to Luisa, who typed everything for me when she wasn't on horseback, to my cats Muschi and Mousie and Birdie and Bunny, my neighbours' cats and all the other cats who crossed my path and were used shamelessly by me as models, my whippets Hasi and Tabby, who managed to sneak into this cat book… and lastly, and most importantly, my brother, Niki, for putting the book together so brilliantly.

Contents

To a Cat

ALGERNON CHARLES SWINBURNE

Stately, kindly, lordly friend
Condescend
Here to sit by me, and turn
Glorious eyes that smile and burn,
Golden eyes, love's lustrous meed,
On the golden page I read.

All your wondrous wealth of hair
Dark and fair,
Silken-shaggy, soft and bright
As the clouds and beams of night,
Pays my reverent hand's caress
Back with friendlier gentleness.

Dogs may fawn on all and some
As they come;
You, a friend of loftier mind,
Answer friends alone in kind.
Just your foot upon my hand
Softly bids it understand.

"All your wondrous wealth of hair dark and fair..."

A Poet's Cat

WILLIAM COWPER

A poet's cat, sedate and grave
As poet well could wish to have,
Was much addicted to inquire
For nooks to which she might retire,
And where secure as mouse in chink,
She might repose, or sit and think.
I know not where she caught the trick -
Nature perhaps herself had cast her
In such a mould philosophique,
Or else she learn'd it of her master.

"She might repose, or sit and think."

From

Dick Barker's Cat

MARK TWAIN

Tom Quartz… knowed more about mining, that cat did, than any man I ever, ever see. You couldn't tell him noth'n' 'bout placer-diggin's – 'n'as for pocket-mining, why he was just born for it. He would dig out after me an' Jim when we went over the hills prospect'n', and he would trot along behind us for as much as five mile, if we went so fur. An' he had the best judgment about mining-ground – why, you never see anything like it. When we went to work, he'd scatter a glance round, 'n' if he didn't think much of the indications, he would give a look as much as to say, "Well, I'll have to get you to excuse me" – 'n' without another word he'd hyste his nose in the air 'n' shove for home. But if the ground suited him, he would lay low 'n' keep dark till the first pan was washed, 'n' then he would sidle up 'n' take a look, an' if there was about six or seven grains of gold he was satisfied – he didn't want no better prospect 'n' that – 'n' then he would lay down on our coats and snore like a steamboat till we'd struck the pocket, an' then get up 'n' superintend. He was nearly lightin' on superintending. Well, by an' by, up comes this yer quartz excitement. Everybody was into it – everybody was pick'n' 'n' blast'n instead of shovellin' dirt on the hillside - everybody was putt'n' down a shaft instead of scrapin' the surface. Noth'n' would do Jim, but we must tackle the ledges, too, 'n' so we did. We commenced putt'n' down a shaft, 'n' Tom Quartz he begin to wonder what in the dickens it was all about. He hadn't ever seen any mining like that before, 'n' he was all

"… the ornieriest-lookin' beast…"

upset, as you may say – he couldn't come to a right understanding of it no way – it was too many for him. He was down on it too, you bet you – he was down on it powerful – 'n' always appeared to consider the cussedest foolishness out. But that cat, you know, was always agin' new-fangled arrangements – somehow he never could abide 'em. You know how it is with old habits. But by an' by Tom Quartz begin to git sort of reconciled a little though he never could altogether understand that eternal sinkin' of a shaft an' never pannin' out anything. At last he got to comin' down in the shaft, hisself, to try to cipher it out. An' when he'd git the blues, 'n' fell kind o' scruffy, 'n' aggravated 'n' disgusted – knowin' as he did, that the bills was runnin' up all the time an' we warn't makin' a cent – he would curl up on a gunny-sack in the corner an' go to sleep. Well, one day when the shaft was down about eight foot, the rock got so hard that we had to put in a blast – the first blast'n we'd ever done since Tom Quartz was born. An' then we lit the fuse 'n' clumb out 'n' got off 'bout fifty yards – 'n' forgot 'n' left Tom Quartz sound asleep on the gunny-sack. In 'bout a minute we seen a puff of smoke bust up out of the hole, 'n' then everything let go with an awful crash, 'n' about four million ton of rocks 'n' dirt 'n' smoke 'n' splinters shot up 'bout a mile an' a half into the air, an' by George, right in the dead center of it was Tom Quartz a-goin' end over end, an' a-snortin' an' a-sneez'n, an' a-clawin' an' a-reach'n' for things like all possessed. But it warn't no use, you know, it warn't no use. An' that was the last we see of him for about two minutes 'n' a half, an' then all of a sudden it begin to rain rocks and rubbage an' directly he come down ker-whoop about ten foot off f'm where we stood. Well, I reckon he was p'raps the orneriest-lookin' beast you ever see. One ear was sot back on his neck, 'n' his tail was stove up, 'n' his eye-winkers were singed off, 'n' he was all blacked up with powder an' smoke, an' all sloppy with mud 'n' slush f'm one end to the other. Well, sir, it warn't no use to try to apologize – we couldn't say a word. He took a sort of disgusted look at hisself 'n' then he looked at us – an' it was just exactly the same as if he had said – "Gents, maybe you think it's smart to take advantage of a cat that ain't had no experience of quartz-minin', but I think different"- an' then he turned on his heel 'n' marched off home without ever saying another word.

Mice and Cat

from

AESOP'S FABLES

The mice all met together one day, very secretly in a safe, dry cellar, to talk about Cat. They had been having a dreadful time lately. Cat was always on the prowl. It seemed that mistress gave him no food and little milk, so that he hunted the mice all day and night. They never had a moment's peace. Only last night he had killed no fewer than five of them. So you can understand that the meeting of mice was a very angry one; if the cellar had not been such a safe cellar, Cat would certainly have heard their angry squeakings.

"I suggest," said one mouse, "that we all live down here. Cat doesn't seem to know about this place."

"That's all very well," said another, "but we've got to go out sometimes and look for food."

"Suppose we move to a different house?" said a third mouse.

"Yes, but which?" someone objected. "There are plenty of mice in most of the houses round here, and they won't welcome us!"

"Besides, there's good eating here."

"Yes, we're used to it. This is our home! Why should we move? Let Cat move."

"That's right," said several mice. "Let's get rid of Cat."

"Poison his milk!" said one mouse.

"...he hunted the mice all day and night."

"Set fire to his tail!" suggested another.

"Attack him all together, and bite him to pieces!"

The meeting was getting nowhere, and the mice had become very disorderly, as well as noisy. Then the smallest mouse of all hopped on to an old flowerpot so that he could be seen, and piped up in a high nervous voice:

"May I speak, p-please? I think I've got an idea."

One mouse laughed, but another said, "Go on, young 'un!" and others said, "Let him speak" and "Quiet, everyone!" and "Out with it, then!"

The very smallest mouse cleared his throat and began.

"The trouble is," he said, "we never know when Cat's coming. He's so quiet and stealthy, he just creeps up on us before we catch sight or smell of him."

"That's right. But how can we help it?"

"Quiet, you, and let the little 'un go on!"

"Well," went on the smallest mouse, "I know where there's a rusty old bell. It's not very big, but it makes a good clear ring when you shake it. I know 'cos me and my sister plays with it sometimes. Well, I thought that if we were to tie that bell round Cat's neck so that he couldn't get it off, we'd always know when he was coming, and we could get out of the way in time."

This seemed to be a wonderful idea. Why had no one thought of it before? Of course! Tie a bell to Cat, and he would never trouble them any more. There was loud cheering and squeaking for joy, and everyone shouted "Hooray! That's the best idea so far. Let's have a vote on it!" And several mice shook the smallest mouse by the paw and slapped him on the back till he was quite dazed and fell off the flowerpot.

"Very well," shouted the most important mouse, rapping on the floor with a nutshell, "Let's take a vote. Paws up for tying a bell round Cat's neck!"

"Just one moment," said the very oldest mouse, getting shakily to his feet and speaking to the meeting for the first time. So far he had just sat quietly in a corner. He was very old and very grey, and all the mice knew he was extremely wise, except when he was asleep, as he nearly always was.

"I think," said he, "this is an excellent plan. If we could attach a bell to our enemy, we should indeed, as our young friend has pointed out, be warned of his approach and be able to get away in time. But before we vote on this proposal, there is just one question I should like to ask – and I think we ought to consider it most carefully."

"Out with it!" said a mouse. "Get it off your chest, Gaffer!"

The oldest mouse took no notice of the interruption, for being rather deaf, he had scarcely heard it.

"Which one of you," he went on, speaking slowly and gravely – "which of you is going to tie this bell round Cat's neck?"

Nobody said a word. There was not a sound. You could have heard a corn-seed drop.

"Dash my whiskers!" thought the smallest mouse to himself. "I never thought of that."

As for the oldest mouse of all, he sat down again in his corner, and fell asleep immediately.

And to this very day, mice have never known how to get the better of Cat.

Before deciding on a plan, find out if it can be carried out.

The Cat Horoscope

MICHAELA FRIEDERIKE

"Lively, a little wild..."

ARIES (March 21 - April 20)

Lively, a little wild and foolhardy. These cats go everywhere, indoors or out and don't care about the consequences. They'll settle down where it suits them, in your home or your garden without a second thought. This is not an arrogant cat, but rather one which is truly independent and confident and definitely selfish! If it were human it would phone you at 3 o'clock in the morning without a word of apology.

Best Owners: Sagittarius or Leo (either totally relaxed or seriously authoritative).
Famous Arians: Charlie Chaplin, Eric Clapton, Vincent van Gogh, Goya, Haydn, Houdini, Elton John, Leonardo da Vinci, Tennessee Williams.

Milk For the Cat

HAROLD MUNRO

"The little black cat with bright green eyes"

When tea is brought at five o'clock,
And all the neat curtains are drawn with care,
The little black cat with bright green eyes
Is suddenly purring there.
At first she pretends, to having nothing to do,
She has come in merely to blink by the grate,
But, though tea may be late and the milk may be sour,
She is never late.
And presently her agate eyes
Take a soft large milky haze,
And her independent casual glance
Becomes a stiff hard gaze.

Then she stamps her claws or lifts her ears
Or twists her tail and begins to stir,
Till suddenly all her lithe body becomes
One breathing trembling purr.
The children eat and wriggle and laugh;
The two old ladies stroke their silk:
But the cat is grown small and thin with desire,
Transformed to a creeping lust for milk.

The white saucer like some full moon descends
At last from the clouds of the table above;
She sighs and dreams and thrills and glows,
Transfigured with love.
She nestles over the shining rim,
Buries her chin in the creamy sea;
Her tail hangs loose; each drowsy paw
Is doubled under each bending knee.
A long dim ecstasy holds her life;
Her world is an infinite shapeless white,
Till her tongue has curled the last holy drop,
Then she sinks back into the night,
Draws and dips her body to heap
Her sleepy nerves in the great arm-chair,
Lies defeated and buried deep
Three or four hours unconscious there.

Calvin the Cat

CHARLES DUDLEY WARNER

"He walked into her house one day out of the great unknown..."

Calvin is dead. His life, long to him, but short to the rest of us, was not marked by startling adventures, but his character was so uncommon and his qualities were so worthy of imitation that I have been asked by those who personally knew him to set down my recollections of his career. His origins and ancestry were shrouded in mystery; even his age was a matter of pure conjecture. Although he was of the Maltese race, I have reason to suppose that he was American by birth as he certainly was in sympathy. Calvin was given to me eight years ago by Mrs. Stowe, but she knew nothing of his age or origin. He walked into her house one day out of the great unknown and became at once at home, as if he had been always a friend of the family. He appeared to have artistic and literary tastes, and it was as if he had enquired at the door if this was the residence of the author of Uncle Tom's Cabin and, upon being assured that it was, had decided to dwell there. This is, of course, fanciful, for his antecedents were wholly unknown, but in his time he could hardly have been in any household where he would not have heard Uncle Tom's Cabin talked about.

When he came to Mrs. Stowe, he was as large as he ever was, and apparently as old as he ever became. Yet there was in him no appearance of age, he was in the happy maturity of all his powers and you would rather have said, in that maturity, he had found the secret of perpetual youth. And it was as difficult to believe that he would ever be aged as it was to imagine that he had ever been in immature youth. There was in him a mysterious perpetuity.

After some years, when Mrs. Stowe made her winter home in Florida, Calvin came to live with us. From the first moment he fell in with the ways of the house and assumed a recognised position in the family – I say recognised, because after he became known he was always enquired for by visitors, and in letters from other members of the family he always received a message. Although the least obtrusive of beings, his individuality always made itself felt. His personal appearance had much to do with this, for he

"...he was of royal mould and had an air of high breeding".

was of royal mould and had an air of high breeding. He was large, but he had nothing of the fat grossness of the celebrated Angora family; though powerful, he was exquisitely proportioned and as graceful in every movement as a young leopard. When he stood up to open a door – he opened all doors with old-fashioned latches – he was portentously tall, and when he stretched on the rug before the fire he seemed too long for this world – as indeed he was. His coat was the finest and softest I have ever seen, a shade of quiet Maltese; and from his throat downwards, underneath, to the white tips of his feet, he wore the whitest and most delicate ermine; and no person was ever more fastidiously neat. In his finely formed head you saw something of his aristocratic character; the ears were small and cleanly cut, there was a tinge of pink in the nostrils, his face was handsome and the expression of his countenance exceedingly intelligent – I should even call it a sweet expression if the term were not inconsistent with his look of alertness and sagacity.

It is difficult to convey a just idea of his gaiety in connection with his dignity and gravity, which his name expressed. As we know nothing of his family, of course it will be understood that Calvin was his Christian name. He had times of relaxation into utter playfulness, delighting in a ball of yarn, catching sportively at stray ribbons when his mistress was at her toilet, and pursuing his own tail, with hilarity, for lack of anything better. He could amuse himself by the hour, and he did not care for children; perhaps something in his past was present to his memory. He had absolutely no bad habits, and his disposition was perfect. I never saw him exactly angry, though I have seen his tail grow to an enormous size when a strange cat appeared on his lawn. He disliked cats, evidently regarding them as feline and treacherous, and he had no association with them. Occasionally there would be heard a night concert in the shrubbery. Calvin would ask to have the door opened, and then you would hear a rush and a 'petzt', and the concert would explode, and Calvin would quietly come in and resume his seat on the hearth. There was no trace of anger in his manner, but he wouldn't have any of that about the house.

He had the rare virtue of magnanimity. Although he had fixed notions about his own rights, and extraordinary persistency in getting them, he never showed temper at a repulse; he simply and firmly persisted till he had what he wanted. His diet was one point; his idea was that of scholars about dictionaries – 'to get the best'. He knew as well as anyone what was in the house, and would refuse beef if turkey was to be had; and if there were oysters, he would wait over turkey to see if the oysters would not be forthcoming. And yet he was not a gross gourmand; he would eat bread if he saw me eating it, and thought he was not being imposed on. His habits of feeding, also, were refined; he never used a knife, and he would put his hand up and draw the fork down to his mouth as gracefully as a grown person. Unless necessity compelled, he would not eat in the kitchen, but insisted upon his meals in the dining-room, and would sit patiently, unless a stranger were present; and then he was sure to importune the visitor, hoping that the latter was ignorant of the rule of house, and would give him something. They used to say that he preferred as his tablecloth on the floor a certain well-known Church journal; but this was said by an Episcopalian.

So far as I know, he had no religious prejudices, except that he did not like the association with Romanists. He tolerated the servants, because they belonged to the house, and would sometimes linger by the kitchen stove; but the moment visitors came in he arose, opened the door and marched into the drawing-room. Yet he enjoyed the company of his equals, and never withdrew, no matter how many callers – whom he recognised as of his society – might come into the drawing-room. Calvin was fond of company, but he wanted to choose it; and I have no doubt that his was an aristocratic fastidiousness rather than one of faith. It is so with most people.

The intelligence of Calvin was something phenomenal, in his rank of life. He established a method of communicating his wants, and even some of his sentiments; and he could help himself in many things. There was a furnace register in a retired room, where he used to go when he wished to

"…his fondness for nature."

be alone, that he always opened when he desired more heat, but never shut it, any more than he shut the door after himself. He could do almost everything but speak; and you would sometimes declare that you could see a pathetic longing to do that in his intelligent face. I have no desire to overdraw his qualities but, if there was one thing in him more noticeable than another, it was his fondness for nature. He could content himself for hours at a low window, looking into the ravine and at the great trees, noting the smallest stir there; he delighted above all things, to accompany me walking about the garden, hearing the birds, getting the smell of fresh earth, and rejoicing in the sunshine. He followed me and gambolled like a dog, rolling over on the turf and exhibiting his delight in a hundred ways. If I worked, he sat and watched me, or looked off over the bank and kept his ear open to the twitter of cherry trees. When it stormed, he was sure to sit at the windows, keenly watching the rain or snow, glancing up and down at its falling; and a winter tempest always delighted him.

I think he was genuinely fond of birds but, so far as I know, confined himself to one a day; he never killed, as some sportsmen do, for the sake of killing, but only as civilised people do – from necessity. He was intimate with the flying-squirrels who dwelt in the chestnut tree – too intimate, for almost every day in the summer he would bring in one, until he nearly discouraged them. He was, indeed, a superb hunter, and would have been a devastating one if the bump of his destructiveness had not been offset by the bump of his moderation. There was little of the brutality of the lower animals about him; I don't think he enjoyed rats for themselves, but he knew his business and, for the first few months of his residence with us, waged an awful campaign against the horde and, after that, his simple presence seemed to deter them from coming on the premises. Mice amused him, but he usually considered

"I don't think he enjoyed rats for themselves, but he knew his business..."

them too small game to be taken seriously; I have seen him play for an hour with a mouse and then let him go with a royal condescension. In this whole manner of 'getting a living' Calvin was a great contrast to the rapacity of the age in which he lived.

I hesitate to speak of his capacity for friendship and the affectionateness of his nature, for I know from his own reserve that he would not care to have it talked about. We understood each other perfectly, but we never made any

"He never forgot his dignity."

fuss about it; when I spoke his name and snapped my fingers, he came to me; when I returned home at night, he was pretty sure to be waiting for me near the gate, and would rise and saunter along the walk, as if his being there was purely accidental – so shy was he commonly of showing feeling; and when I opened the door he never rushed in, like a cat, but loitered and lounged, as if he had no intention of going in, but would condescend to. And yet, the fact was, he knew dinner was ready and he was bound to be there. He kept the run of dinner-time. It happened sometimes, during our absence in the summer, that dinner would be early, and Calvin, walking about the grounds, missed it and came in late. But he never made the mistake a second day.

There was one thing he never did – he never rushed through an open doorway. He never forgot his dignity. If he had to ask to have the door opened, and was eager to go out, he always went deliberately; I can see him now standing on the sill, looking about at the sky as if he were thinking whether it were worth taking an umbrella, until he was near having his tail shut in.

His friendship was rather constant than demonstrative. When we returned from an absence of nearly two years Calvin welcomed us with evident pleasure, but showed his satisfaction rather by tranquil happiness than by fuming about. He had the faculty of making us glad to get home. It was his constancy that was so attractive. He liked companionship, but he wouldn't be petted, or fussed over, or sit in anyone's lap a moment; he always extricated himself from such familiarity with dignity and with no show of temper. If there was any petting to be done, however, he chose to do it. Often he would sit looking at me and then, moved by a delicate affection, come and pull at my coat and sleeve until he could touch my face with his nose, and then go away contented. He had a habit of coming to my study in the morning sitting quietly by my side or on the table for hours, watching the pen run over the paper, occasionally swinging his tail round for a blotter and then going to sleep among the papers by the inkstand. Or, more rarely, he would watch the writing from a perch on my shoulder. Writing always interested him and, until he understood it, he wanted to hold the pen.

He always held himself in a kind of reserve with his friend, as if he had said, "Let's respect our personality and not make a 'mess' of friendship." He saw, with Emerson, the risk of degrading it to trivial conveniency. "Why insist on rash personal relations with your friends. Leave this touching and clinging." Yet I would not give an unfair notion of his aloofness, his fine sense of the sacredness of the me and the not-me. And, at the risk of not being believed, I will relate an incident which was often repeated. Calvin had the practice of passing a portion of the night in the contemplation of its beauties and would come into our chamber over the roof of the conservatory through the open window, summer and winter, and go to sleep at he foot of my bed. He would do this always exactly in this way; he was never content to stay in the chamber if we compelled him to go up the stairs and through the door. He had the obstinacy of General Grant. But this is by the way. In the morning he performed his toilet and went down to breakfast with the rest of the family. Now, when the mistress was absent from home, and at no other time, Calvin would come up in the morning, when the bell rang, to the head of the bed, put up his feet and look into my face, follow me about when I rose, 'assist' at my dressing, and in many purring ways show his fondness, as if he had plainly said, "I know that she has gone away, but I am here." Such was Calvin in rare moments.

He had his limitations. Whatever passion he had for nature, he had no conception of art. There was sent to him once a fine and very expressive cat's head in bronze, by Frémiet. I placed it on the floor. He regarded it intently, approached it cautiously and crouching, touched it with his nose, perceived the fraud, turned away abruptly and would never notice it afterwards.

On the whole, his life was not only a successful one, but a happy one. He never had but one fear, so far as I know; he had a mortal and a reasonable terror of plumbers. He would never stay in the house when they were here. No coaxing could quiet him. Of course he didn't share our fear about their charges, but he must have had some dreadful experience with them in that portion of his life which is unknown to us. A plumber was to him the devil,

"In the morning he performed his toilet..."

and I have no doubt that, in his scheme, plumbers were foreordained to do him mischief.

In speaking of his worth, it has never occurred to me to estimate Calvin by worldly standards. I know that it is customary now, when anyone dies, to ask how much he was worth, and that no obituary in the newspapers is considered complete without such an estimate. The plumbers in our house were one day overheard to say that "They say that she says that he says he wouldn't take $100 for him." It is unnecessary to say that I never made such

"…the bay-window in the dining-room…"

a remark, and that, so far as Calvin was concerned, there was no purchase in money.

As I look back upon it, Calvin's life seems to me a fortunate one, for it was natural and unforced. He ate when he was hungry, slept when he was sleepy, and enjoyed existence to the very tips of his toes and to the end of his expressive and slow-moving tail. He delighted to roam about the garden, and stroll among the trees, and to lie on the green grass and luxuriate in all the sweet influences of summer. You could never accuse him of idleness, and yet he knew the secret of repose. The poet who wrote so prettily of him that his little life was rounded with a sleep understated his felicity; it was rounded with a good many. His conscience never seemed to interfere with his slumbers. In fact, he had good habits and a contented mind. I can see him now walk in at the study door, sit down by my chair, bring his tail artistically about his feet, and look up at me with unspeakable happiness in his handsome face.

I often thought that he felt the dumb limitation which denied him the power of language. But since he was denied speech, he scorned the inarticulate mouthings of the lower animals. The vulgar mewing and yowling of the cat species was beneath him; he sometimes uttered a sort of articulate and well-bred ejaculation, when he wished to call attention to something that he considered remarkable, or to some want of his, but he never went whining about. He would sit for hours at a closed window, when he desired to enter, without a murmur, and when it was opened he never admitted that he had been impatient by 'bolting' in. Though speech he had not, and the unpleasant kind of utterance given to his race he would not use, he had a mighty power of purr to express his measureless content with congenial society. There was in him a musical organ with stops of varied power and expression, upon which I have no doubt that he could have performed Scarlatti's celebrated cat's fugue.

Whether Calvin died of old age, or was carried off by one of the diseases incident to youth, it is impossible to say; for his departure was as quiet as his advent was mysterious. I only know that he had appeared to us in the world in his perfect stature and beauty, and that after a time, like Lohengrin, he withdrew. In his illness there was nothing more to be regretted than in all his blameless life. I suppose there was never an illness that had more dignity and sweetness and resignation in it. It came on gradually, in a kind of listlessness and loss of appetite. An alarming symptom was his preference for the warmth of a furnace register to the lively sparkle of an open wood fire. Whatever pain he suffered, he bore it in silence, and seemed only anxious not to obtrude his malady. We tempted him with the delicacies of the season, but it soon became impossible for him to eat, and for two weeks he ate and drank scarcely anything. Sometimes he made the effort to take something, but it was evident that he made the effort to please us. The neighbours – and I am convinced that the advice of neighbours is never good for anything – suggested catnip. He wouldn't even smell it. We had the attendance of an amateur practitioner of medicine, whose real office was the cure of souls, but nothing touched his case. He took what was offered, but it was with the air of one to whom the time for pellets was passed. He sat or lay day after day almost motionless, never once making a display of those vulgar convulsions or contortions of pain which are so disagreeable to society. His favourite place was on the brightest spot of a Smyrna rug by the conservatory, where the sunlight fell and he could hear the fountain play. If we went to him and exhibited our interest in his condition, he always purred in recognition of our sympathy. And when I spoke his name, he looked up with an expression that said, "I understand it, old fellow, but it's no use." He was to all who came to visit him a model of calmness and patience in affliction.

I was absent from home at the last, but heard by daily postal card of his failing condition and never again saw him alive. One sunny morning he rose from his rug, went into the conservatory (he was very thin then), walked around it deliberately, looking at all the plants he knew, and then went to the bay-window in the dining-room and stood a long time looking out at the little field, now brown and sere, and towards the garden where perhaps the happiest hours of his life had been spent. It was a last look. He turned and walked away, laid himself down on the bright spot on the rug, and quietly died.

It is not too much to say that a little shock went through the neigbourhood when it was known that Calvin was dead, so marked was his individuality; and his friends, one after another, came in to see him. There was no sentimental nonsense about his obsequies; it was felt that any parade would have been distasteful to him. John, who acted as undertaker, prepared a candle-box for him, and I believe assumed a professional decorum; but there may have been the usual levity underneath, for I heard that he remarked in the kitchen that it was the 'driest wake he ever attended'. Everybody, however, felt a fondness for Calvin, and regarded him with a certain respect. Between him and Bertha there existed a great friendship, and she apprehended his nature; she used to say that sometimes she was afraid of him, he looked at her so intelligently; she was never certain that he was what he appeared to be.

When I returned, they had laid Calvin on a table in an upper chamber by an open window. It was February. He reposed in a candle-box, lined about the edges with evergreen, and at his head stood a little wine glass with flowers. He lay with his head tucked down in his arms – a favourite position of his before the fire – as if asleep in the comfort of his soft and exquisite fur. It was the involuntary exclamation of those who saw him, "How natural he looks!" As for myself I said nothing. John buried him under the twin hawthorn trees – one white and the other pink – in a spot where Calvin was fond of lying and listening to the hum of summer insects and the twitter of birds.

Perhaps I have failed to make appear the individuality of character that was so evident to those who knew him. At any rate, I have set down nothing concerning him but the literal truth. He was always a mystery. I did not know whence he came; I do not know whither he has gone. I would not weave one spray of falsehood in the wreath I lay upon his grave.

A Cat in Arcadia

SIR PHILIP SYDNEY

"...eye of fire..."

I have (and long shall have) a white great nimble cat,
A king upon a mouse, a strong foe to the rat,
Fine eares, long taile he hath, with Lions curbed clawe,
Which oft he lifteth up, and stayes his lifted pawe,
Deepe musing to himselfe, which after-mewing showes,
Till with lickt beard, his eye of fire espie his foes.

The Cat Horoscope

MICHAELA FRIEDERIKE

"He's quite unflappable."

TAURUS (April 21 - May 21)

This is the cat which is always under your feet, because nothing bothers him or seems to concern him. He's quite unflappable. Put a bomb under him and he won't care or even notice. The John Wayne of the cat world, the strong and silent type; doesn't waste his words or his affections until he really gets close to you.

Best Owners: Cancer (consistent and reliable despite superficial mood swings).

Famous Taureans: Oliver Cromwell, Salvador Dali, Queen Elizabeth II, Sigmund Freud, Willie Nelson, Florence Nightingale, William Shakespeare.

Little White King

MARGUERITE STEEN

"All remarked on his beauty."

Spring vanished with the blossom, and summer loitered imperceptibly into autumn. The sycamores clung to their leaves, then, in two or three sudden gusts, let them down on the lawns. He found a new delight: that of following the gardener as he swung the arc of the broom across and across the grass. Sometimes he became a white windmill, a catherine wheel of silver, cutting indescribable capers among the dry brown flakes that broke into confetti on his back, his flanks and the banner of his tail. Always addicted to the mower, he helped to give the lawns their last cut of the year.

All who had known him from his infancy remarked on the burgeoning of his beauty, during those autumnal weeks. 'In standing water' between kitten and cat, his adolescence, like that of the human animal, had a poignancy of its own, which one knew must vanish when his transformation was complete. He had grown enormously; from the tip of his nose to the base of his tail he was already longer than the Black One, although not quite so tall. The tail had lost the last of its pale golden trace, and was broader than the broadest ostrich plume. His feet no longer seemed too big for his body, and had garnished themselves with a set of powerful nails, more like jade than ivory, which he still employed too often on the upholstery, but never on those who played with him. If, by misfortune, they missed their mark – the piece of ribbon or paper or string we were trailing for him – and registered on human flesh, it was never his intention; the torn hand, offered in place of the toy, was patted with a pad of velvet.

He was very imperious; very definite and autocratic in his requirements. He really needed a vassal, dedicated to his service alone: to shut and open doors, give him a drop of milk, dry his paws when he had been out in the rain, find the ping-pong balls he always batted into the most inaccessible places, or carry him on a shoulder. Although it was easy to say he was 'always eating' (a couple of mouthfuls at a time), no thickness developed in the soft elastic body, no hardness in the tender bones. To lift him was still like lifting a muff. I wondered how long the sweet sensation would last. He must harden, grow sinewy, develop the rangy stride of the male and the predatory head of the hunter. Of one thing I was glad: the loss of his sex had not affected his vocal cords; his cry, his purr still had the richness of the entire.

One thing in particular endeared him to me: his almost benign attitude towards birds. Full of interest and curiosity, he stalked them, but never – in my sight at least – attempted to kill them. He followed the foolish feathered things through grass or border, flattening himself, watching with sparkling eyes, but never, apparently, with lethal intent. He appeared to extend to

"…field mice…"

them the innocent attention he gave to all small moving objects – leaves, butterflies or shadows. He leapt, he struck. If the blow ever landed, one can hardly doubt that primitive instinct would have asserted itself; but somehow, for all his agility, he always missed, and, missing, lost interest in the game.

The same with field mice. Never having had to hunt for his food, he was content to give them a pat or two, and could seldom be troubled to follow them when they escaped into the long grass. I must confess to feeling rather badly about this: something like a mother whose small boy fails to distinguish himself in the field of sport; but consoled myself by reflecting on his many gifts and graces, which more sportsmanlike cats could not rival.

"...on the dining-room hearthrug..."

I remembered one of my little North Country queens, a loving little party, who almost every morning brought me in a cold, dead mouse, which she laid on my pillow and nuzzled affectionately up against my ear, in case I should overlook it; it was a compliment with which one could dispense – and one which may well have occurred to le Petit Roi if he had been a mouser. I had been spared something – if only the sight of mutilated little bodies, which, vermin though they be, give me a horrid pang.

When winter declared itself, with fogs and frosts and raw, cheerless mornings, he spent more time indoors, making still closer acquaintance of the human beings who guarded his simple life.

He had no specially favoured spot for his repose; sometimes it was at the head of the stairs, close to a radiator. Sometimes it was on the dining-room hearthrug, in front of the Pither stove, or on one of the Napoleon chairs in the corners of the fireside. On sunny mornings it was in the deep alcove of a little window, between the Frank Dobson model of a child's head and the sun-warmed glass. Sometimes it was the dressing stool in front of my looking glass with the electric stove behind him. At night, when we gathered in the parlour, it was the back of a couch, or under the flounce of a chair. Unlike the Black One, he did not care for cushions or any too yielding surface; I had learned when he came on my bed, to push back the eiderdown and make a little flat space for him to sleep on the mattress, where, after conducting his toilet, he settled to sleep.

One thing he had in common with the Black One: a mania for the social life. Christmas, with an influx of guests, was bliss – from the dinner party on Christmas Eve to the Twelfth Night cocktail. It was not only a wild and whirling time of tinsel and cellophane, sparkles and ribbons, things that went bang and flashed (his first experience of drawing room fireworks brought him near swooning point with ecstasy); but he was the centre of attention – the Snow King, the Winter King, le petit roi Noël!

He received tributes with dignified reserve, resisted some foolish attempts to interest him in his Christmas cards and, sated at last with pleasure, folded his paws under his chest, to watch the goings-on. His best Christmas present, a mechanical mouse, he played with on Christmas Eve, showing, I fear, more politeness than enthusiasm, and thereafter abandoned. Human beings, with their strange and unpredictable antics, were more fun than a clockwork mouse. His aloofness made the Black One's eager friendliness and her readiness to show off her few self-taught tricks appear – alas – almost fulsome.

He and the Black One had arrived, by then, at 'an understanding'. It was his doing, not hers. But she, with all her elderly ways, her natural anxiety

"Christmas, with an influx of guests, was bliss…"

to retain the first place in my affection, was not averse to a little pink muzzle that lifted itself to hers. The warmth and comfort of that silver fleece on a winter night. They had begun occasionally to share an armchair: the Black One reluctant, taut, drawn into herself and stiff with resistance, he folded calmly, seemingly immovable, but encroaching little by little on her space, on the woollen scarf that belonged to her, until their limbs were touching. The Black One flung agonised glances at me: "Must I bear this?" I nodded. The Black One sighed and accepted the all but imperceptible contact. She drew the line, however, on the one occasion he attempted to wash her. What? – a miniature poodle with four champions in her pedigree – submit to being washed by a cat? She bit him, for once, in earnest – and justifiably; and the lesson did him no harm. He sat, blinking offendedly; but, in that respect, he sinned no more. Even when he chewed the tassels on her ears, he showed, thereafter, a certain awareness of 'thus far and no further' – which he was keen enough on claiming for himself.

As the days darkened, and there was little to tempt him out of doors, he developed a regime of his own. In the mornings he shadowed Alice about her household duties. Sometimes on her shoulder, sometimes under her arm, he helped her to dust, to sweep and polish – pouncing with delight on the duster, taking flying leaps on to the tops of cupboards or dressers; finally settling on plate-chest or sideboard, his tail curled round his toes, admiring his own reflection in the shining surface. When he endangered something fragile or precious with his antics, Alice's reproachful "Bert!" was an endearment. When I picked him up in my arms, and, instead of giving him the spanking he had earned, called him "My white tom kitten!" his struggles and flounces to escape were tolerated for the sake of his perfect beauty.

One of the things most beguiling, to cat-lovers, is the intractability of a cat, its blank refusal of coercion, its refusal to surrender the least part of its spiritual independence even for those for whom it has learned to care. No one who does not understand and accept this is fit to have the guardianship of a cat. Only one cat of my acquaintance, a Mrs. Bertha Mocatta, was amenable to physical punishment; but Mrs. B. was a gorgeous old tavern harridan who took from her owner the cosh she constantly earned as merely one of the courtesies of everyday existence, and was capable to her last breath of fighting back. Idolizing the hand that obliged her to behave herself,

Mrs. B. was one of the immortals; for some time after her demise, her presence was (literally) felt in the studio over which she ruled after her previous owners gave up the local in which she was raised. Her ghost would still be around, I think, but for the establishment of her successor, the gentle Mrs. Laura Chevely, against whom ghostly teeth and ghostly talons cannot prevail.

It may be noticed that I use the word 'guardianship' in preference to 'ownership,' of a cat. 'Ownership' implies authority over body and soul. A dog, in its devotion, will, of its own free will, accept this authority; a cat, never. This independence is offensive to people who do not care for cats: I have never been able to understand why. I can no more see why one should assume possession over an animal than over a human being.

Now that winter had come, le Petit Roi's afternoons were passed in sleep, unless a brief gleam of sun enticed him out of doors, or the northerly gale, fluttering the dead leaves, tempted him to fling himself about the lawns. He would visit our neighbours, trotting across their grass, lifting his head, uttering his beguiling Prr-rr-oo, and wave his tail in acknowledgement of a caress, before leaping up to their pergola, or on the garage roof, or into the pear tree, where he stood out on a branch, noble as the ship's figurehead breasting the gale; or, up on the ridge tiles, allowed himself to be blown into a white chrysanthemum by the wind.

His communications with those who shared the house with him now notably increased their range. When he looked up and observed "Prr-rr-oo", he was not asking for food, or to go out, or to be played with. It was "I am here"; or "Where have you been?" or simply "Take notice of me." Often he came and sat beside me, on the arm of chair or sofa, purring so loudly that the Black One would rouse and lift her head in astonishment.

He discovered the miracle of fires; tempting as they were, he was very sensible about them. For all the comfort they gave him, he was careful not to singe his coat or the restless plume of his tail. And, cosy as he found them, he would withdraw himself – though with an air of protest – if the person he wished to be with was not sitting near the fire.

In one manner he was implacable, and, as the evening wore on, impatient. He must have his games. Useless to offer him his ping-pong balls, his string with the rabbit's tail on the end of it, his crumpled bits of silver paper or the bell that swung on the Black One's collar and lead. He flatly refused to play by himself. He sulked, setting up a protestant yowl; leapt on the card table, to scatter aces and kings and queens, and to pat the pencil of the score card onto the floor. Dismissed as a nuisance, he set out on a gloomy progress over chairs, tables and sofas; he deliberately attacked the screen of cordobes leather, or the newly covered couch – anything that was precious and would bring some one leaping to check his ill behaviour.

There was nothing to do but to play with him; to rush up and down stairs, trailing a scarf, or the Black One's lead. The game hurtled from room to room; he crouched under beds, to leap out with a wild pat at our ankles; he flung himself prone in affected exhaustion belied by the wild, dark brightness of his eyes. Sometimes the exhaustion was real, and he submitted to being thrown over one's shoulder like a white tippet, and rocked backwards and forwards, purring quietly – until, at the moment one fondly believed he was falling asleep, he would take a bound like a flying squirrel, and the game was on again.

One day shortly after Christmas he had a shock.

At twilight, I opened the back door to let him out, and as he took a cautious step onto the porch, the air around him filled itself with white feathers. The whirling whiteness took him by surprise; he drew back, then, losing his head completely, turned round and flew straight up into my arms. I laughed and held him, and walked out with him on to the path. The snow fell on him and me, and because I was holding him he recovered his confidence, and presently leapt lightly down and went to his accustomed place on the border. But for once he did not linger. It was too cold. He flashed past me, rushed to the drawing room fire, and began hurriedly to lick the cold wetness that had settled on his coat.

Next morning, sitting on the bench at my bedroom window, he looked out on a strange world: a scene of whiteness, glittering with sun. He was fascinated. Presently he called to be let out, and slid onto the back porch, which had been swept clear, and was already warmed by the eastern sun. He sat there, taking in the altered aspects of his familiar surroundings. After watching le Petit Roi gazing at the greenness which overnight had been translated into whiteness, I have no doubt that cats know about colour. He was baffled and impressed.

The flagged path that leads down under the archway and out into the lane had also been swept, and at his own leisure, he trotted down it, for another view of this strange, white scene.

Meanwhile the Black One had gone for her morning walk. She had known many snows and, on the whole, enjoyed them. Her minute feet, hardly bigger than birds' claws, sank into the cold softness, she rubbed her muzzle in the snow and came up with white moustaches and fringes of white on her ears. As le Petit Roi sat there, under the arches, she returned up the lane.

He rose on his toes; he blew himself out into a white balloon; he spat – for the first time in his life. He swayed back into a defensive arc, as IT came by: a black and yellow IT, familiar, yet horribly strange. The Black One, in her daffodil-yellow sweater which he had never seen before, horrified him. He slapped out a paw. The Black One stood still and stared. He hunched himself, let out a slow, protracted growl, and spat again. The Black One, impressed, walked up for a closer view of this strange conduct on the part of one who, so far, had never been anything but amiable.

His eyes blackened and enlarged themselves, his pink mouth, wide open, dragged back at the corners, held in his breath. Then with a gasp, he recognised the Black One, and shot like an arrow for the kitchen door. Shaking the snow from her fringes, the Black One galloped after him. They hunched at each other in front of the dining-room stove, then spent ten minutes smelling each other all over from head to tail, as though meeting for the first time.

That was the week he discovered the possibilities of the Knole couch. The last, most lovely picture of the Little King is of a long white arm, reaching between the back and the slung end of the couch; of a snow-white head, mad with gaiety, and a pair of ruby-red eyes blazing from the shadow at the evening paper, rolled up and poked into the space between cushions and wall for him to snatch at. It was round about that time that I wrote in my diary:

"Of all the cats that have owned me, there has never been one like my white tom kitten, for sweetness, intelligence and affection. Hearing is very unimportant, after all."

Choosing their Names

THOMAS HOOD

"Our old cat has kittens three"

Our old cat has kittens three –
What do you think their names should be?

One is tabby with emerald eyes,
And a tail that is long and slender,
And into a temper she quickly flies
If you ever by chance offend her.
I think we shall call her this -
I think we shall call her that –
Now don't you think Pepperpot
Is a nice name for a cat?

One is black with a frill of white,
And her feet are all white fur,
If you stroke her she carries her tail upright
And quickly begins to purr.
I think we shall call her this -
I think we shall call her that –
Now don't you think Sootikin
Is a nice name for a cat?

One is a tortoiseshell yellow and black,
With plenty of white about him;
If you tease him, at once he sets up his back,
He's a quarrelsome one, ne'er doubt him.
I think we shall call him this -
I think we shall call him that–
Now don't you think that Scratchaway
Is a nice name for a cat?

Our old cat has kittens three
And I fancy what their names will be:
Pepperpot, Sootikin, Scratchaway – there!
Were there ever kittens with these to compare?
And we call the old mother –
Now what do you think? –
Tabitha Longclaws Tiddley Wink.

From

The History of
Four-Footed Beasts

EDWARD TOPSELL

It is reported that the flesh of cats salted and sweetened hath power in it to draw wens from the body, and being warmed to cure the Hemmorhoids and pains in the veins and back, according to the verse of Ursinus. In Spain and Gallia Norbon, they eat cats, but first of all take away their head and tail, and hang the prepared flesh a night or two in the open cold air, to exhale the savour of it, finding the flesh thereof almost as sweet as a cony. The flesh of cats can seldom be free from poison, by reason of their daily food, eating Rats and Mice, Wrens and other birds which feed on poison, and above all the brain of the Cat is most venomous, for it being above all measure dry, stoppeth the animal spirits, that they cannot pass into the venticle, by reason thereof memory faileth, and the infected person falleth into a Phrenzie. The hair also of a cat being eaten unawares, stoppeth the artery and causeth suffocation. To conclude this point it appeareth that this is a dangerous beast, and that therefore as for necessity we are constrained to nourish them for the suppressing of small vermin: so with a wary eye we must avoid their harms, making more account of their use than of their persons.

"Wrens and other birds..."

The Cat Horoscope

MICHAELA FRIEDERIKE

"Would as soon watch a bird as kill it."

GEMINI (May 22 - June 21)

Two cats in one; sunshine and showers; a living contradiction and never a dull moment! Would as soon watch a bird as kill it. This is a cat, who, even as a grown-up, will take pleasure in attacking your shoelaces or gently flicking the pencil off your desk and onto the floor. Can sometimes appear a little demanding of your time and attention.

Best Owners: Libra (introverted, artistic, controlled...a perfect complement to the extrovert Gemini), Aquarius, (friendly, peace-loving, unconventional).
Famous Geminis: Dante, Bob Dylan, Clint Eastwood, Paul Gaugin, J.F. Kennedy, Henry Kissinger, Marilyn Monroe, Cole Porter, Stravinsky.

The Owl and the Pussycat

EDWARD LEAR

The owl and the pussycat went to sea
In a beautiful pea-green boat:
They took some honey and plenty of money
Wrapped up in a five-pound note.
The Owl looked up to the stars above,
And sang to a small guitar,
"O lovely Pussy, O Pussy my love,
What a beautiful Pussy you are,
You are,
You are!
What a beautiful Pussy you are!"

Said Pussy to Owl, "You elegant fowl,
How charmingly sweet you sing!
Oh! Let us be married: too long we have tarried:
But what shall we do for a ring?"
They sailed away, for a year and a day,
To a land where the bong-tree grows:
And there in a wood a Piggy-wig stood,
With a ring at the end of his nose,
His nose,
His nose,
With a ring at the end of his nose.

"Dear Pig, are you willing to sell for one shilling
Your ring?" Said the Piggy "I will."
So they took it away, and were married next day
By the turkey who lives on the hill.
They dined on mince and slices of quince
Which they ate with a runcible spoon;
And hand in hand, on the edge of the sand,
They danced by the light of the moon,
The moon,
The moon,
They danced by the light of the moon.

"The owl and the pussycat…"

From

Through the Looking-Glass and What Alice Found There

LEWIS CARROLL

One thing was certain, that the white kitten had had nothing to do with it: it was the black kitten's fault entirely. For the white kitten had been having its face washed by the old cat for the last quarter of an hour (and bearing it pretty well, considering); so you see it couldn't have had any hand in the mischief.

The way Dinah washed her children's faces was this: first she held the poor thing down by its ear with one paw, and then with the other paw she rubbed its face all over, the wrong way; beginning at the nose: and just now, as I said, she was hard at work on the white kitten, which was lying quite still and trying to purr – no doubt feeling that it was all meant for its good.

But the black kitten had been finished with earlier in the afternoon, and so, while Alice was sitting curled up in a corner of the great arm-chair, half talking to herself and half asleep, the kitten had been having a grand game of romps with the ball of worsted Alice had been trying to wind up, and had been rolling it up and down till it had all come undone again; and there it was, spread over the hearth-rug, all knots and tangles, with the kitten running after its own tail in the middle.

"Oh, you wicked little thing!" cried Alice, catching up the kitten, and giving it a quick kiss to make it understand that it was in disgrace. "Really, Dinah ought to have taught you better manners! You ought, Dinah, you know you ought!" she added, looking reproachfully at the old cat, and speaking in as cross a voice as she could manage – and then she scrambled back into the arm-chair, taking the kitten and worsted with her, and began winding up the ball again. But she didn't get on very fast, as she was talking all the time, sometimes to the kitten, and sometimes to herself. Kitty sat very demurely on her knee, pretending to watch the progress of the winding, and now and then putting out one paw and gently touching the ball, as if it would be glad to help if it might.

"Do you know what to-morrow is, Kitty?" Alice began. "You'd have guessed if you'd been up in the window with me – only Dinah was making you tidy, so you couldn't. I was watching the boys getting in sticks for the bonfire – and it wants plenty of sticks, Kitty! Only it got so cold, and it snowed so, they had to leave off. Never mind, Kitty, we'll go and see the bonfire to-morrow." Here Alice wound two or three turns of the worsted round the kitten's neck, just to see how it would look: this lead to a scramble, in which the ball rolled down upon the floor, and yards and yards of it got unwound again.

"Do you know, I was so angry, Kitty," Alice went on, as soon as they were comfortably settled again, "when I saw all the mischief you had been doing, I was very nearly opening the window, and putting you out in the snow! And you'd have deserved it, you little mischievous darling! What have you got to say for yourself? Now don't interrupt me!" she went on, holding up one finger. "I'm going to tell you all your faults. Number one: you squeaked twice while Dinah was washing your face this morning. Now you

"I was very nearly opening the window, and putting you out in the snow!"

can't deny it, Kitty, for I heard you! What's that you say?" (pretending that the kitten was speaking.) "Her paw went into your eye? Well, that's your fault, for keeping your eyes open – if you'd shut them tight up, it wouldn't have happened. Now don't make any more excuses, but listen! Number two: you pulled Snowdrop away by the tail just as I had put down the saucer of milk before her! What, you were thirsty, were you? How do you know she wasn't thirsty too? Now for number three: you unwound every bit of the worsted while I wasn't looking!"

"That's three faults, Kitty, and you've not been punished for any of them yet. You know I'm saving up all your punishment for Wednesday week – suppose they had saved up all my punishments!" she went on, talking more to herself than the kitten. "What would they do at the end of a year? I should be sent off to prison, I suppose, when the day came. Or – let me see – suppose each punishment was to be going without a dinner: then, when the miserable day came, I should have to go without fifty dinners at once! Well I shouldn't mind that much! I'd far rather go without them than eat them!"

From

Five Hundredth Good Pointes of Husbandrie

(September)

THOMAS TUSSER

Provide against Michaelmas, bargaine to make,
for farmer to give over, to keepe or to take:
In doing of either, let wit beare a stroke,
for buying or selling, of a pig in a poke.

Thomas Tusser is warning his 16th Century readers not to be taken in by fraudsters selling a pig in a "poke" (a sack or bag). The problem was that the unscrupulous were known to sometimes put a cat instead of a pig into the bag. The unwary farmer would part with his cash and go home with a bag thought to contain a sucking-pig to fatten up for the Christmas table, when in fact the bag contained a cat, which was (at least in those days) a much less valuable animal! By the time the farmer discovered the fraud the seller would have been long gone. Tusser says you can avoid this by using your "wit" . If you look carefully at what you're buying you will "let the cat out of the bag", thus exposing the fraud.

"...a bag thought to contain a sucking-pig...
when in fact the bag contained a cat..."

Ode on the Death of a Favourite Cat, Drowned in a Tub of Gold Fishes

THOMAS GRAY

"Her coat, that with the tortoise vies…"

'Twas on a lofty vase's side
Where China's gayest art had dyed
The azure flowers, that blow;
Demurest of the tabby kind, The pensive Selima, reclined,
Gazed on the lake below.

Her conscious tail her joy declared;
The fair round face, the snowy beard,
The velvet of her paws,
Her coat, that with the tortoise vies,
Her ears of jet, and emerald eyes,
She saw; and purr'd applause.

Still had she gazed; but 'midst the tide
Two angel forms were seen to glide,
The genii of the stream:
Their scaly armour's Tyrian hue
Through richest purple to the view
Betray'd a golden gleam.

The hapless nymph with wonder saw:
A whisker first, and then a claw,
With many an ardent wish,
She stretch'd, in vain, to reach the prize.
What female heart can gold despise?
What cat's averse to fish?

Presumptuous maid! With looks intent
Again she stretch'd, again she bent,
Nor knew the gulf between.
(Malignant Fate sat by, and smiled)
The slipp'ry verge her feet beguiled,
She tumbled headlong in.

Eight times emerging from the flood
She mew'd to ev'ry wat'ry God,
Some speedy aid to send.
No Dolphin came, no Nereid stirr'd:
Nor cruel Tom, nor Susan heard.
A fav'rite has no friend!

From hence, ye beauties, undeceived,
Know, one false step is ne'er retrieved,
And be with caution bold.
Not all that tempts your wand'ring eyes
And heedless hearts is lawful prize,
Nor all that glitters, gold.

From

Alice in Wonderland

LEWIS CARROLL

"The cat only grinned when it saw Alice..."

The cat only grinned when it saw Alice. It looked good-natured, she thought: still it had very long claws and a great many teeth, so she felt it ought to be treated with respect.

"Cheshire Puss," she began, rather timidly, as she did not at all know whether it would like the name; however, it only grinned a little wider. "Come, it's pleased so far," thought Alice, and she went on. "Would you tell me, please, which way I ought to go from here?"

"That depends a good deal on where you want to get to," said the Cat.

"I don't much care where –" said Alice.

"Then it doesn't matter which way you go," said the Cat.

" – so long as I get somewhere," Alice added as an explanation.

"Oh, you're sure to do that," said the Cat. "If you only walk long enough."

Alice felt this could not be denied, so she tried another question. "What sort of people live about here?"

"In that direction," the Cat said, waving its right paw round, "lives a Hatter: and in that direction lives a March Hare. Visit either you like: they're both mad."

"But I don't want to go among mad people," Alice remarked.

"Oh, you can't help that," said the Cat: "we're all mad here. I'm mad. You're mad."

"How do you know I'm mad?" said Alice.

"You must be" said the Cat, "or you wouldn't have come here."

Alice didn't think that proved it at all; however, she went on. "And how do you know that you're mad?"

"To begin with," said the Cat, "a dog's not mad. You grant that?"

"I suppose so," said Alice.

"Well, then," the Cat went on, "you see a dog growls when it's angry, and wags its tail when it's pleased. Now I growl when I'm pleased, and wag my tail when I'm angry. Therefore I'm mad."

"I call it purring, not growling," said Alice.

"Call it what you like," said the Cat. "Do you play croquet with the Queen to-day?"

"I should like it very much," said Alice, "but I haven't been invited yet."

"You'll see me there," said the Cat, and vanished.

Alice was not much surprised at this, she was getting so used to queer things happening. While she was looking at the place where it had been, it suddenly appeared again.

"By-the-bye, what became of the baby?" said the Cat. "I'd nearly forgotten to ask."

"It turned into a pig," Alice quietly said, just as if it had come back in a natural way.

"I thought it would," said the Cat, and vanished again.

Alice waited a little, half expecting to see it again, but it did not appear, and after a minute or two she walked on in the direction in which the March Hare was said to live. "I've seen hatters before," she said to herself; "the March Hare will be much the most interesting, and perhaps, as this is May, it won't be raving mad – at least not so mad as it was in March." As she said this, she looked up, and there was the Cat again, sitting on a branch of a tree.

"Did you say pig, or fig?" said the Cat.

"I said pig," replied Alice; "and I wish you wouldn't keep appearing and vanishing so suddenly: you make one quite giddy."

"All right," said the Cat; and this time it vanished quite slowly, beginning with the end of its tail, and ending with the grin, which remained some time after the rest of it had gone.

"Well! I've often seen a cat without a grin," thought Alice; "but a grin without a cat! It's the most curious thing I ever saw in all my life!"

Cat

ALAN BROWNJOHN

"...an unseen marmalade cat..."

Sometimes I am an unseen
marmalade cat, the friendliest colour,
making off through a window without permission,
pacing along a broken-glass wall to the greenhouse,
jumping down with a soft, four-pawed thump,
finding two inches open of the creaking door
with the loose brass handle,
slipping impossibly in,
flattening my fur at the hush and touch of the sudden warm air,
avoiding the tiled gutter of slow green water,
skirting among the potted nests of tetchy cactuses,
and sitting with my tail flicked
skillfully underneath me, to sniff
the azaleas the azaleas the azaleas.

The Cat Horoscope

MICHAELA FRIEDERIKE

*"One minute he's swinging from the chandelier and
the next he's curled up in the sanctuary of his basket..."*

CANCER (June 22 - July 21)

This is a complicated cat and one of the most difficult for the poor human to understand. One minute he's swinging from the chandelier and the next he's curled up in the sanctuary of his basket or hiding under the bed. Don't expect too much curling up on your lap from this cat.

Best Owners: Pisces (self-confident, creative and don't care what others think of them) Scorpio (controlled, calm, confident...).
Famous Cancers: Louis Armstrong, Julius Caesar, Henry VIII, Nelson Mandela, Brian May, Marcel Proust, Rasputin, Rembrandt, Ringo Starr.

My Boss the Cat

PAUL GALLICO

If you are thinking about acquiring a cat at your house and you would care for a quick sketch of what your life would be like under Felix domesticus, you have come to the right party. I have figured out that, to date, I have worked for – and I mean worked for – thirty-nine of these four-legged characters, including one memorable period when I was doing the bidding of some twenty-three assorted resident felines all at the same time.

Cats are, of course, no good. They're chisellers and panhandlers, sharpers and shameless flatterers. They are as full of schemes and plans, plots and counterplots, wiles and guiles as any confidence man. They can read your character better than a $50-an-hour psychiatrist. They know to a milligram how much of the old oil to pour on to break you down. They are definitely smarter than I am, which is one reason why I love 'em.

Cat-haters will try to floor you with the old argument, "If cats are so smart, why can't they do tricks, the way dogs do?" It isn't that cats can't do tricks; it's that they won't. They're far to hep to stand up and beg for food when they know in advance that you'll give it to them anyway. And as for rolling over, or playing dead, or 'speaking', what's in it for pussy that isn't already hers?

Cats, incidentally, are a great warm-up for a successful marriage – they teach you your place in the household. The first thing Kitty does is to organise your home on a comfortable basis – her basis. She'll eat when she wants to; she'll go out at her pleasure. She'll come in when she gets good and ready, if at all. She wants attention when she wants it and darn well means to be let alone when she has other things on her mind. She is jealous; she won't have you showering attentions or caresses on other minxes, whether two or four-footed.

"…I have worked for thirty-nine of these four-legged characters.…"

She gets upset when you come home late and when you go away on a business trip. But when she decides to stay out a couple of nights, it is none of your darned business where she's been or what she's been up to. Either you trust her or you don't.

"She'll come in when she gets good and ready..."

She hates dirt, bad smells, poor food, loud noises and people you bring home unexpectedly to dinner.

Kitty also has her share of small-child obstinacy. She enjoys seeing you flustered, fussed, red in the face and losing your temper. Sometimes, as she hangs about watching, you get the feeling that it is all she can do to keep from busting out laughing. And she's got the darndest knack for putting the entire responsibility for everything on you.

For instance, Kitty pretends that she can neither talk nor understand you, and that she is therefore nothing but a poor dumb animal. What a laugh! Any self-respecting racket-working cat can make you understand at all times exactly what she wants. She has one voice for "Lets eat", another for wanting out, still a third for "You don't happen to have seen my toy mouse around here, the one with the tail chewed off?" and a host of other easily identified speeches. She can also understand you perfectly, if she thinks there's profit in it.

I once had a cat I suspected of being able to read. This was a gent named Morris, a big tabby with topaz eyes who lived with me when I was batching it in a New York apartment. One day I had just finished writing to a lady who at that time was the object of my devotion. Naturally I brought considerable of the writer's art into telling her this. I was called down to the telephone for a few minutes. When I returned, Morris was sitting on my desk reading the letter. At least, he was staring down at it looking a little ill. He gave me that long baffled look of which cats are capable, and immediately meowed to be let out. He didn't come back for three days. Thereafter I kept my private correspondence locked up.

The incident reminds me of another highly discriminating cat I had down on the farm by the name of Tante Hedwig. One Sunday a guest asked me whether I could make a cocktail called a Mexican. I said I thought I could, and proceeded to blend a horror of gin, pineapple juice, vermouth, bitters and other ill-assorted ingredients. Pouring out a trial glass, I spilled it on the grass. Tante Hedwig came over, sniffed, and with a look of shameful embarrassment solicitously covered it over. Everybody agreed later that she had something there.

Let me warn you not to put too much stock in the theory that animals do not think and that they only act by instinct. Did you ever try to keep a cat out that wanted to come in, or vice versa? I once locked a cat in the cellar. He climbed a straight cement wall, hung on with his paws (I saw the claw marks to prove it), unfastened the window-hook with his nose and climbed out.

Cats have fabulous memories, I maintain, and also the ability to measure and evaluate what they remember. Take, for instance, our two Ukrainian greys, Chin and Chilla. My wife brought them up on a medicine dropper. We gave them love and care and a good home on a farm in New Jersey.

Eventually we had to travel abroad, so Chin and Chilla went to live with friends in Glenview, Ill., a pretty snazzy place. Back in the United States we went out to spend Thanksgiving in Glenview. We looked forward, among other things, to seeing our two cats. When we arrived at the house, Chin and Chilla were squatting at the top of a broad flight of stairs. As we called up a tender greeting to them, we saw an expression of horror come over their faces. "Great heavens! It's those paupers! Run!" With that, they vanished and could not be found for five hours. They were frightened to death we had come to take them back to the squalor of a country estate in New Jersey, and deprive them of a room of their own in Illinois, with glassed-

"...another highly discriminating cat I had down on the farm..."

in sun porch, screens for their toilets and similar super-luxuries. After a time they made a grudging appearance and consented to play the old games and talk over old times, guardedly. But when the hour arrived for our departure they vanished once more. Our hostess later wrote to us that apparently they got hold of a timetable and waited until our train was past Elkhart before coming out.

It was this same cat Chilla who, one day on the farm after our big ginger cat, Wuzzy, had been missing for forty-eight hours, led us to where he was, a half a mile away, out of sight and out of hearing, caught in a trap. Every so often Chilla would look back to see if we were coming. Old Wuzz was half dead when we got there, but when he saw Chilla he started to purr.

Two-Timing, or Leading the Double Life, is something you may be called upon to face with your cat. It means simply that Kitty manages to divide her time between two homes sufficiently far apart that each home-owner thinks she is his.

I discovered this when trying to check up on the unaccountable absences of Lulu II, a seal-point Siamese. I finally located her at the other end of the bay, mooching on an amiable spinster. When I said, "Oh, I hope my Lulu hasn't been imposing on you," she replied indignantly, "Your Lulu! You mean our dear little Pitipoo! We've been wondering where she went when she disappeared occasionally. We do hope she hasn't been annoying you."

The shocking part of this story, of course, is that for the sake of a handout, Lulu, with a pedigree as long as your arm, was willing to submit to being called Pitipoo.

Of all the things a smart cat does to whip you into line, the gift of a captured mouse is the cleverest and most touching. There was Limpy, the wild barn cat down on the farm who lived off what she caught in the fields. We were already supporting four cats, but in the winter, when we went to town, we brought her along. We had not been inside the apartment ten minutes before Limpy caught a mouse, or probably the mouse, and at once brought it over and laid it at our feet. Now, as indicated before, Limpy had hunted to survive. To Limpy, a dead mouse was Big and Little Casino, a touchdown, home run and Grand Slam. Yet this one she gave to us.

"...the wild barn cat..."

How can you mark it up except as rent, or thanks, or "Here, looka; this is the most important thing I can do. You take it because I like you? You can teach a dog to retrieve and bring you game, but only a cat will voluntarily hand over its kill to you as an unsolicited gift."

How come Kitty acts not like the beast of prey she is but like a better-class human being? I don't know the answer. The point is, she does it – and makes you her slave ever after. Once you have been presented with a mouse by your cat, you will never be the same again. She can use you for a door-mat. And she will, too.

Bright Ribbons

ALAN DEVOE

"We tie bright ribbons round their necks…"

We tie bright ribbons round their necks, and occasionally little tinkling bells, and we affect to think that they are as sweet and vapid as the coy name 'Kitty' by which we call them would imply. It is a curious illusion. For, purring beside our fireplaces and pattering along our back fences, we have got a wild beast as uncowed and uncorrupted as any under heaven.

A Cat

JULIE BROWN

"A cat is a little bag of fur..."

A cat is a little bag of fur
Filled with a heart and lots of purr.

The Cat Horoscope

MICHAELA FRIEDERIKE

"...a look of distinct superiority..."

LEO (July 22 - August 22)

Leo the lion, king of the jungle, top dog (so to speak...). He strides through his territory (his, not yours...) with his nose in the air and a look of distinct superiority on his imperturbably regal face. You'd better know your place with this cat and humour him in his belief that he really does rule the world.

Best Owners: Anyone except Gemini (too extrovert) or Capricorn (too ambitious, calculating and selfish to be dominated by a Leo-cat...).
Famous Leos: Fidel Castro, Henry Ford, Alfred Hitchcock, Mick Jagger, Madonna, Napoleon, Rasputin, Percy Bysshe Shelley, Andy Warhol.

Wave-silk Tabby

JOY FLINT

Textured Tabby,
Contemplating,
Textile lands
Beneath his paws.

Grey and rain-swept,
Northern Tabby,
Dreaming of
His Eastern land.

Northern Tabby,
Warm in firelight,
Takes the road
To Samarkand.

Eastern Tabby,
On the shoreline,
Burning sand
Beneath his paws.

"...Textile lands beneath his paws."

Contemplating,
Eastern Tabby,
Scale-bright fish
On orient sands.

Eastern Tabby,
Patient dreamer,
Stretches out
One silken paw.

Compleat Angler,
Eastern Tabby,
Fishing out
His glittering prize.

Northern Tabby's
Golden journey
Sea-horse, shrimp
And lobster finds.

Making patterns,
Northern Tabby,
Weaves in bones
Around his head.

Textured Tabby,
Wave-silk Tabby,
Lost in lands
Beneath his paws.

From

Life of Dr Samuel Johnson

JAMES BOSWELL

I shall never forget the indulgence with which he treated Hodge, his cat; for whom he himself used to go out and buy oysters, lest the servants having that trouble should take a dislike to the poor creature. I am, unluckily, one of those who have an antipathy to a cat, so that I am uneasy when in the room with one; and I own, I frequently suffered a good deal from the presence of the same Hodge. I recollect him one day scrambling up Dr Johnson's breast, apparently with much satisfaction, while my friend, smiling and half-whistling, rubbed down his back, and pulled him by the tail; and when I observed he was a fine cat, saying, "Why, yes, Sir, but I have had cats whom I liked better than this"; and then, as if perceiving Hodge to be out of countenance, adding, "but he is a very fine cat, a very fine cat indeed."

"…a very fine cat indeed."

The Story of Webster

PG WODEHOUSE

"Cats are not dogs!"

"Cats are not dogs!"

There is only one place where you can hear good things like that thrown off quite casually in the general run of conversation, and that is the bar parlour of the *'Angler's Rest'*. It was there, as we sat grouped about the fire, that a thoughtful Pint of Bitter had made the statement just recorded.

Although the talk up to that point had been dealing with Einstein's Theory of Relativity, we readily adjusted our minds to cope with the new topic. Regular attendance at the nightly sessions over which Mr Mulliner presides with such unfailing dignity and geniality tends to produce such mental nimbleness. In our little circle I have known an argument on the Final Destination of the Soul to change inside forty seconds into one concerning the best method of preserving the juiciness of bacon fat.

"Cats", proceeded the Pint of Bitter," are selfish. A man waits on a cat hand and foot for weeks, humouring its lightest whim, and then it goes and leaves him flat because it has found a place down the road where the fish is more frequent."

"What I've got against cats", said a Lemon Sour, speaking feelingly, as one brooding on a private grievance, "is their unreliability. They lack candour and are not square shooters. You get your cat and you call him Thomas or George, as the case may be. So far, so good. Then one morning you wake up and find six kittens in the hat-box and you have to reopen the whole matter, approaching it from an entirely different angle."

"If you want to know what's the trouble with cats," said a red-faced man with glassy eyes, who had been rapping on the table with his forth whisky, "they've got no tact. That's what's the trouble with them. I remember a friend of mine had a cat. Made quite a pet of that cat, he did. And what occurred? What was the outcome? One night he came home late and was feeling for the keyhole with his corkscrew; and believe me or not, his cat selected that precise moment to jump on the back of his neck out of a tree. No tact."

Mr Mulliner shook his head.

"I grant you all this," he said, "but still, in my opinion, you have not got to the root of the matter. The real objection to the great majority of cats is their insufferable air of superiority. Cats, as a class, have never completely got over the snootiness caused by the fact that in Ancient Egypt they were worshipped as gods. This makes them far too prone to set themselves up as critics and censors of the frail and erring human beings whose lot they share. They stare rebukingly. They view with concern. And on a sensitive man this often has the worst effects, including an inferiority complex of the gravest kind. It is odd that the conversation should have taken this turn," said Mr Mulliner, sipping his hot Scotch and lemon, "for I was thinking only this afternoon of the rather strange case of my cousin Edward's son, Lancelot."

"I knew a cat —" began a small Bass.

My cousin Edward's son, Lancelot (said Mr Mulliner) was at the time I speak, a comely youth of some twenty-five summers. Orphaned at an early age, he had been brought up in the home of his Uncle Theodore, the saintly Dean of Bolsover; and it was a great shock to that good man when Lancelot, on attaining his majority, wrote to inform him that he had taken a studio in Bott Street, Chelsea, and proposed to remain in the metropolis and become an artist.

The Dean's opinion of artists was low. As a prominent member of the Bolsover Watch Committee, it had recently been his distasteful duty to be present at a private showing of the super-super- film, *Palettes of Passion*; and he replied to his nephew's communication with a vibrant letter in which he emphasized the grievous pain it gave him to think that one of his flesh and blood should deliberately be embarking on a career which must inevitably lead sooner or later to the painting of Russian princesses lying on divans in the semi-nude with their arms round tame jaguars. He urged Lancelot to return and become a curate while there was yet time.

"...their insufferable air of superiority."

But Lancelot was firm. He deplored the rift between himself and a relative whom he had always respected; but he was dashed if he meant to go back to an environment where his individuality had been stifled and his soul confined in chains. And for four years there was silence between uncle and nephew.

During these years Lancelot had made progress in his chosen profession. At the time at which this story opens, his prospects seemed bright. He was painting the portrait of Brenda, only daughter of Mr and Mrs B. B. Carberry-Pirbright, of 11 Maxton Square, South Kensington, which meant thirty pounds in his sock on delivery. He had learned to cook bacon and eggs. He had practically mastered the ukulele. And, in addition, he was engaged to be married to a fearless young vers libre poetess of the name of Gladys Bingley, better known as The Sweet Singer of Garbridge Mews, Fulham – a charming girl who looked like a pen-wiper.

It seemed to Lancelot that life was very full and beautiful. He lived joyously in the present, giving no thought to the past.

But how true it is that the past is inextricably mixed up with the present and that we can never tell when it may spring some delayed bomb beneath our feet. One afternoon, as he sat making a few small alterations to the portrait of Brenda Carberry-Pirbright, his fiancée entered.

He had been expecting her to call, for today she was going off for a three weeks' holiday to the South of France, and she had promised to look in on her way to the station. He laid down his brush and gazed at her with a yearning affection, thinking for the thousandth time how he worshipped every spot of ink on her nose. Standing there in the doorway with her bobbed hair sticking out in every direction like a golliwog's, she made a picture that seemed to speak to his very depths.

"Hullo, Reptile!" he said lovingly.

"What ho, Worm!" said Gladys, maidenly devotion shining through the monocle which she wore in her left eye. "I can stay just half an hour."

"Oh well, half an hour soon passes," said Lancelot. "What's that you've got there?"

"A letter, ass. What did you think it was?"

"Where did you get it?"

"I found the postman outside."

Lancelot took the envelope from her and examined it.

"Gosh!" he said.

"What's the matter?"

"It's from my Uncle Theodore."

"I didn't know you had an Uncle Theodore."

"Of course I have. I've had him for years."

"What's he writing to you about?"

"If you'll kindly keep quiet for two seconds, if you know how," said Lancelot, "I'll tell you."

And in a clear voice which, like that of all the Mulliners, however distant from the main branch, was beautifully modulated, he read as follows:

> *The Deanery,*
> *Bolsover, Wilts.*

My Dear Lancelot,

As you have, no doubt, already learned from your Church Times, *I have been offered and have accepted the vacant Bishopric of Bongo-Bongo, in West Africa. I sail immediately to take up my new duties, which I trust will be blessed.*

In these circumstances it becomes necessary for me to find a good home for my cat Webster. It is, alas, out of the question that he should accompany me, as the rigours of the climate and the lack of essential comforts might well sap a constitution which has never been robust.

I am dispatching him, therefore, to your address, my dear boy, in a straw-lined hamper, in the full confidence that you will prove a kindly and conscientious host.

With cordial good wishes,
> *Your affectionate uncle,*
> *THEODORE BONGO-BONGO*

For some moments after he had finished reading this communication, a thoughtful silence prevailed in the studio. Finally Gladys spoke.

"Of all the nerve!" she said. "I wouldn't do it."

"Why not?"

"What do you want with a cat?"

Lancelot reflected.

"It is true," he said, "that, given a free hand, I would prefer not to have my studio turned into a cattery or cat-bin. But consider the special circumstances. Relations between Uncle Theodore and self have for the last few years been a bit strained. In fact, you might say we have definitely parted brass-rags. It looks to me as if he were coming round. I should describe this letter as more or less what you might call an olive-branch. If I lush this cat up satisfactorily, shall I not be in a position later on to make a swift touch?"

"He is rich, this bean?" said Gladys, interested.

"Extremely."

"Then," said Gladys, "consider my objections withdrawn. A good stout cheque from a grateful cat-fancier would undoubtedly come in very handy. We might be able to get married this year."

"Exactly," said Lancelot. "A pretty loathsome prospect, of course; but still, as we've arranged to do it, the sooner we get it over, the better, what?"

"Absolutely."

"Then that's settled. I accept custody of the cat."

"It's the only thing to do," said Gladys. "Meanwhile, can you lend me a comb? Do you have such a thing in your bedroom?"

"What do you want with a comb?"

"I got some soup in my hair at lunch. I won't be a minute."

She hurried out, and Lancelot, taking up the letter again, found he had omitted to read a continuation of it on the back page.

It was to the following effect:

PS. In establishing Webster in your home, I am actuated by another motive than the simple desire to see to it that my faithful friend and companion is adequately provided for.

From both a moral and an educative standpoint, I am convinced that Webster's society will prove of inestimable value to you. His advent, indeed, I venture to hope, will be a turning-point in your life. Thrown, as you must be, incessantly among loose and immoral Bohemians, you will find this cat an example of upright conduct which cannot but act as an antidote to the poison cup of temptation which is, no doubt, hotly pressed to your lips.

PPS. Cream only at midday, and fish not more than three times a week.

He was reading these words for the second time, when the front door-bell rang and he found a man on the steps with a hamper. A discreet mew from within revealed its contents, and Lancelot, carrying it into the studio, cut the strings.

"Hi!" he bellowed, going to the door.

"What's up?" shrieked his betrothed from above.

"The cat's come."

"All right. I'll be down in a jiffy."

Lancelot returned to the studio.

"What ho, Webster!" he said cheerily. "How's the boy?"

The cat did not reply. It was sitting with bent head, performing that wash and brush up which a journey by rail renders so necessary.

In order to facilitate these toilet operations, it had raised its left leg and was holding it rigidly in the air. And there flashed into Lancelot's mind an old superstition handed onto him, for what it was worth, by one of the nurses from his infancy. If, this woman had said, you creep up to a cat when its leg is in the air and give it a pull, then you make a wish and your wish comes true in thirty days.

It was a pretty fancy, and it seemed to Lancelot that the theory might as well be put to the test. He advanced warily, therefore, and was in the act of extending his fingers for the pull, when Webster, lowering the leg, turned and raised his eyes.

He looked at Lancelot. And suddenly with sickening force there came to Lancelot the realization of the unpardonable liberty he had been about to take.

Until this moment, though the postscript to his uncle's letter should have warned him, Lancelot Mulliner had had no suspicion of what manner of cat this was that he had taken into his home. Now for the first time, he saw him steadily and saw him whole.

Webster was very large and very black and very composed. He conveyed the impression of being a cat of deep reserves. Descendant of a long line of ecclesiastical ancestors who had conducted their decorous courtships beneath the shadow of cathedrals and on the back walls of bishops' palaces, he had that exquisite poise which one sees in high dignitaries of the Church. His eyes were clear and steady, and seemed to pierce to the very roots of the young man's soul, filling him with a sense of guilt.

Once, long ago, in his hot childhood, Lancelot, spending his summer holidays at the Deanery, had been so far carried away by ginger-beer and original sin as to plug a senior canon in the leg with his air-gun – only to

"Webster was very large and very black and very composed."

discover, on turning, that a visiting archdeacon had been a spectator of the entire incident from his immediate rear. As he had felt then, when meeting the archdeacon's eye, so did he feel now as Webster's gaze played silently on him.

Webster, it is true, had not actually raised his eyebrows. But this, Lancelot felt, was simply because he hadn't any.

He backed, blushing.

"Sorry!" he muttered.

There was a pause. Webster continued his steady scrutiny. Lancelot edged towards the door.

"Er – excuse me – just a moment…" he mumbled. And, sidling from the room, he ran distractedly upstairs.

"I say," said Lancelot.

"Now what?" asked Gladys.

"Have you finished with the mirror?"

"Why?"

"Well, I – er – thought," said Lancelot, "that I might have a shave."

The girl looked at him astonished.

"Shave? Why, you only shaved the day before yesterday."

"I know. But, all the same…I mean to say, it only seems respectful. That cat, I mean."

"What about him?"

"Well, he seems to expect it somehow. Nothing actually said, don't you know, but you could tell by his manner. I thought a quick shave and perhaps a change into my blue serge suit –"

"He's probably thirsty. Why don't you give him some milk?"

"Could one, do you think?" said Lancelot doubtful. "I mean, I hardly seem to know him well enough." He paused. "I say, old girl," he went on, with a touch of hesitation.

"Hullo?"

"I know you won't mind me mentioning it, but you've got a few spots of ink on your nose."

"Of course I have. I always have spots of ink on my nose."

"Well…you don't think…a quick scrub with a bit of pumice-stone…

I mean to say, you know how important first impressions are…"

The girl stared.

"Lancelot Mulliner," she said, "if you think I'm going to skin my nose to the bone just to please a mangy cat –"

"Sh!" cried Lancelot, in agony.

"Here, let me go down and look at him," said Gladys petulantly.

As they re-entered the studio, Webster was gazing with an air of quiet distaste at an illustration from *La Vie Parisienne* which adorned one of the walls. Lancelot tore it down hastily.

Gladys looked at Webster in an unfriendly way.

"So that's the blighter!"

"Sh!"

"If you want to know what I think," said Gladys, "that cat's been living too high. Doing himself a dashed sight too well. You'd better cut his rations down a bit."

In substance, her criticism was not unjustified. Certainly, there was about Webster more than a suspicion of embonpoint. He had that air of portly well-being which we associate with those who live in cathedral closes. But Lancelot winced uncomfortably. He had so hoped that Gladys would make a good impression, and here she was, starting right off by saying the tactless thing.

He longed to explain to Webster that it was only her way; that in the Bohemian circles of which she was such an ornament genial chaff of a personal order was accepted and, indeed, relished. But it was too late. The mischief had been done. Webster turned in a pointed manner and withdrew silently behind the Chesterfield.

Gladys, all unconscious, was making preparations for departure.

"Well, bung-ho," she said lightly. "See you in three weeks. I suppose you and that cat'll both be out on the tiles the moment my back's turned."

"Please! Please!" moaned Lancelot. "Please!"

He had caught sight of the tip of a black tail protruding from behind the Chesterfield. It was twitching slightly, and Lancelot could read it like a book. With a sickening sense of dismay, he knew that Webster had formed a snap judgement of his fiancée and condemned her as frivolous and unworthy.

It was some ten days later that Bernard Worple, the neo-Vorticist sculptor, lunching at the Puce Ptarmigan, ran into Rodney Scollop, the powerful young surrealist. And after talking for a while of their art:

"What's all this I hear about Lancelot Mulliner?" asked Worple. "There's a wild story going round that he was seen shaved in the middle of the week. Nothing in it I suppose?"

Scollop looked grave. He had been on the point of mentioning Lancelot himself, for he loved the lad and was deeply exercised about him.

"It's perfectly true," he said.

"It sounds incredible."

Scollop leaned forward. His fine face troubled.

"Shall I tell you something, Worple?"

"What?"

"I know for an absolute fact," said Scollop, "that Lancelot Mulliner now shaves every morning."

Worple pushed aside the spaghetti which he was wreathing about him and through the gap stared at his companion.

"Every morning?"

"Every single morning. I looked in on him myself the other day, and there he was, neatly dressed in blue serge and shaved to the core. And, what is more, I got the distinct impression that he had used talcum powder afterwards."

"You don't mean that!"

"I do. And shall I tell you something else? There was a book lying open on the table. He tried to hide it, but he wasn't quick enough. It was one of those etiquette books!"

"An etiquette book!"

"*Polite Behaviour*, by Constance, Lady Bodbank."

Worple unwound a stray tendril of spaghetti from about his left ear. He was deeply agitated. Like Scollop, he loved Lancelot.

"He'll be dressing for dinner next!"

"I have every reason to believe," said Scollop gravely, "that he does dress for dinner. At any rate, a man closely resembling him was seen furtively buying three stiff collars and a black tie at Hope Brothers in the King's Road last Tuesday."

Worple pushed his chair back, and rose. His manner was determined.

"Scollop," he said, "we are friends of Mulliner's, you and I. It is evident from what you tell me that subversive influences are at work and that never has he needed our friendship more. Shall we not go round and see him immediately?"

"It was what I was about to suggest myself," said Rodney Scollop.

Twenty minutes later they were in Lancelot's studio, and with a significant glance Scollop drew his companion's notice to their host's appearance. Lancelot Mulliner was neatly, even foppishly dressed in blue serge with creases down the trouser-legs, and his chin, Worple saw with a pang, gleamed smoothly in the afternoon light.

At the sight of his friends' cigars, Lancelot exhibited unmistakable concern.

"You don't mind throwing those away, I'm sure," he said pleadingly.

Rodney Scollop drew himself up a little haughtily.

"And since when," he asked, "have the best fourpenny cigars in Chelsea not been good enough for you?"

Lancelot hastened to soothe him.

"It isn't me," he exclaimed. "It's Webster. My cat. I happen to know he objects to tobacco smoke. I had to give up my pipe in deference to his views."

Bernard Worple snorted.

"Are you trying to tell us," he sneered, "that Lancelot Mulliner allows himself to be dictated to by a blasted cat?"

"Hush!" cried Lancelot, trembling. "If you knew how he disapproves of strong language!"

"Where is this cat?" asked Rodney Scollop. "Is that the animal?" he said, pointing out of the window to where, in the yard, a tough-looking Tom with tattered ears stood mewing in a hard-boiled way out of the corners of its mouth.

"Good heavens, no!" said Lancelot. "That is an alley cat which comes round here from time to time to lunch at the dustbin. Webster is quite different. Webster has a natural dignity and repose of manner. Webster is a cat who prides himself on always being well turned out and whose high principles and lofty ideals shine from his eyes like beacon fires..." And then suddenly, with an abrupt change of manner, Lancelot broke down and in a low voice added: "Curse him! Curse him! Curse him! Curse him!"

Worple looked at Scollop. Scollop looked at Worple.

"Come on, old man," said Scollop, laying a gentle hand on Lancelot's

"...in the yard, a tough-looking Tom..."

bowed shoulder. "We are your friends. Confide in us."

Lancelot uttered a bitter, merciless laugh.

"You want to know what's the matter? Listen, then. I'm cat-pecked!"

"Cat-pecked?"

"You've heard of men being hen-pecked, haven't you?" said Lancelot with a touch of irritation. "Well, I'm cat-pecked."

And in broken accents he told his story. He sketched the history of his association with Webster from the latter's first entry into the studio. Confident that the animal was not within earshot, he unbosomed himself without reserve.

"It's something in the beast's eye," he said in a shaking voice. "Something hypnotic. He casts a spell upon me. He gazes at me and disapproves. Little by little, bit by bit, I am degenerating under his influence from a wholesome, self-respecting artist into … well, I don't know what you call it. Suffice it to say that I have given up smoking, that I have ceased to wear carpet slippers and go about without a collar, that I never dream of sitting down to my frugal evening meal without dressing, and" – he choked – "I have sold my ukulele."

"Not that!" said Worple, paling.

"Yes," said Lancelot. "I felt that he considered it frivolous."

"Mulliner," said Scollop, "this is more serious than I had supposed. We must brood upon your case."

"It may be possible," said Worple, "to find a way out."

Lancelot shook his head hopelessly.

"There is no way out. I have explored every avenue. The only thing that could possibly free me from this intolerable bondage would be if once – just once – I could catch that cat unbending. If once – merely once – it would lapse in my presence from its austere dignity for but a single moment, I feel that the spell would be broken. But what hope is there of that?" cried Lancelot passionately. "You were pointing just now to that alley cat in the yard. There stands one who has strained every nerve and spared no effort to break down Webster's self-control. I have heard that animal say things to him which you would think no cat with red-blood in its veins would suffer for an instant. And Webster merely looks at him like a Suffragan Bishop eyeing an erring schoolboy and turns his head and falls into a refreshing sleep."

He broke off with a dry sob. Worple, always an optimist, attempted in his kindly way to minimize the tragedy.

"Ah, well," he said. "It's bad, of course, I suppose there is no actual harm in shaving and dressing for dinner and so on. Many great artists … Whistler, for example –"

"Wait!" cried Lancelot. "You have not heard the worst."

He rose feverishly, and, going to the easel, disclosed the portrait of Brenda Carberry-Pirbright.

"Take a look at that," he said, "and tell me what you think of her."

His two friends surveyed the face before them in silence. Miss Carberry-Pirbright was a young woman of prim and glacial aspect. One sought in vain for her reasons for wanting to have her portrait painted. It would be a most unpleasant thing to have about any house.

Scollop broke the silence.

"Friend of yours?"

"I can't stand the sight of her" said Lancelot vehemently.

"Then," said Scollop, "I may speak frankly. I think she's a pill."

"A blister" said Worple.

"A boil and a disease," said Scollop, summing up.

Lancelot laughed hackingly.

"You have described her to a nicety. She stands for everything most alien to my artist soul. She gives me a pain in the neck. I'm going to marry her."

"What!" cried Scollop.

"But you're going to marry Gladys Bingley," said Worple.

"Webster thinks not," said Lancelot bitterly. "At their first meeting he weighed Gladys in the balance and found her wanting. And the moment he saw Brenda Carberry-Pirbright he stuck his tail up at right angles, uttered a cordial gargle, and rubbed his head against her leg. Then turning, he looked at me. I could read that glance. I knew what was in his mind. From that moment he has been doing everything in his power to arrange the match."

"But, Mulliner," said Worple, always eager to point out the bright side, "why should this girl want to marry a wretched, scrubby, hard-up footer like you? Have courage, Mulliner. It is simply a question of time before you repel and sicken her."

Lancelot shook his head.

"No," he said. "You speak like a true friend, Worple, but you do not understand. Old Ma Carberry-Pirbright, this exhibit's mother, who chaperones her at her sittings, discovered at an early date my relationship to my Uncle Theodore, who, as you know, has got it in gobs. She knows well enough that some day I shall be a rich man. She used to know my Uncle Theodore when he was Vicar of St Botolph's in Knightbridge, and from the very first she assumed towards me the chumminess of an old family friend. She was always trying to lure me to her At Homes, her Sunday luncheons, her little dinners. Once she actually suggested that I should escort her and her beastly daughter to the Royal Academy."

He laughed bitterly. The mordant witticisms of Lancelot Mulliner at the expense of the Royal Academy were quoted from Tite Street in the south to Holland Park in the north and eastward as far as Bloomsbury.

"To all these overtures," resumed Lancelot, "I remained firmly unresponsive. My attitude was one from the start of frigid aloofness. I did not actually say in so many words that I would rather be dead in a ditch than at one of her At Homes, but my manner indicated it. And I was just beginning to think I had choked her off when in crashed Webster and upset everything. Do you know how many times I've been to that infernal house in the last week? Five. Webster seemed to wish it. I tell you, I am a lost man."

He buried his face in his hands. Scollop touched Worple on the arm, and together the two men stole silently out.

"Bad!" said Worple.

"Very bad," said Scollop.

"It seems incredible."

"Oh, no. Cases of this kind are, alas, by no means uncommon among those who, like Mulliner, possess to a marked degree the highly-strung, ultra-artistic temperament. A friend of mine, a rhythmical interior decorator, once rashly consented to put his aunt's parrot up at his studio while she was away visiting friends in the north of England. She was a woman of strong evangelical views, which the bird had imbibed from her. It had a way of putting its head on one side, making a noise like someone drawing a cork from a bottle, and asking my friend if he was saved. To cut a long story short, I happened to call in on him a month later and he had installed a harmonium in his studio and was singing hymns, ancient and modern, in a rich tenor, while the parrot, standing on one leg on its perch, took the bass. A very sad affair. We were all much upset about it."

"...his aunt's parrot..."

Worple shuddered.

"You appall me, Scollop! Is there nothing we can do?"

Rodney Scollop considered for a moment.

"We might wire Gladys Bingley to come home at once. She might possibly reason with the unhappy man. A woman's gentle influence...Yes, we could do that. Look in at the post office on your way home and send

Gladys a telegram. I'll owe you for my half of it."

In the studio they had left, Lancelot Mulliner was staring dumbly at a black shape which had just entered the room. He had the appearance of a man with his back to the wall.

"No!" he was crying. "No! I'm dashed if I do!"

Webster continued to look at him.

"Why should I?" demanded Lancelot weakly.

Webster's gaze did not flicker.

"Oh, all right," said Lancelot sullenly.

He passed from the room with leaden feet, and, proceeding upstairs, changed into morning clothes and a top hat. Then, with a gardenia in his buttonhole, he made his way to 11 Maxton Square, where Mrs Carberry-Pirbright was giving one of her intimate little teas ('just a few friends') to meet Clara Throckmorton Stooge, authoress of *A Strong Man's Kiss*.

Gladys Bingley was lunching at her hotel in Antibes when Worple's telegram arrived. It occasioned her the gravest concern.

Exactly what it was all about she was unable to gather, for emotion had made Bernard Worple rather incoherent. There were moments, reading it, when she fancied that Lancelot had met with a serious accident; others when the solution seemed to be that he had sprained his brain to such an extent that rival lunatic asylums were competing eagerly for his custom; others, again, when Worple appeared to be suggesting that he had gone into partnership with his cat to start a harem. But one fact emerged clearly. Her loved one was in serious trouble of some kind, and his best friends were agreed that only her immediate return could save him.

Gladys did not hesitate. Within half an hour of the receipt of the telegram she had packed her trunk, removed a piece of asparagus from her

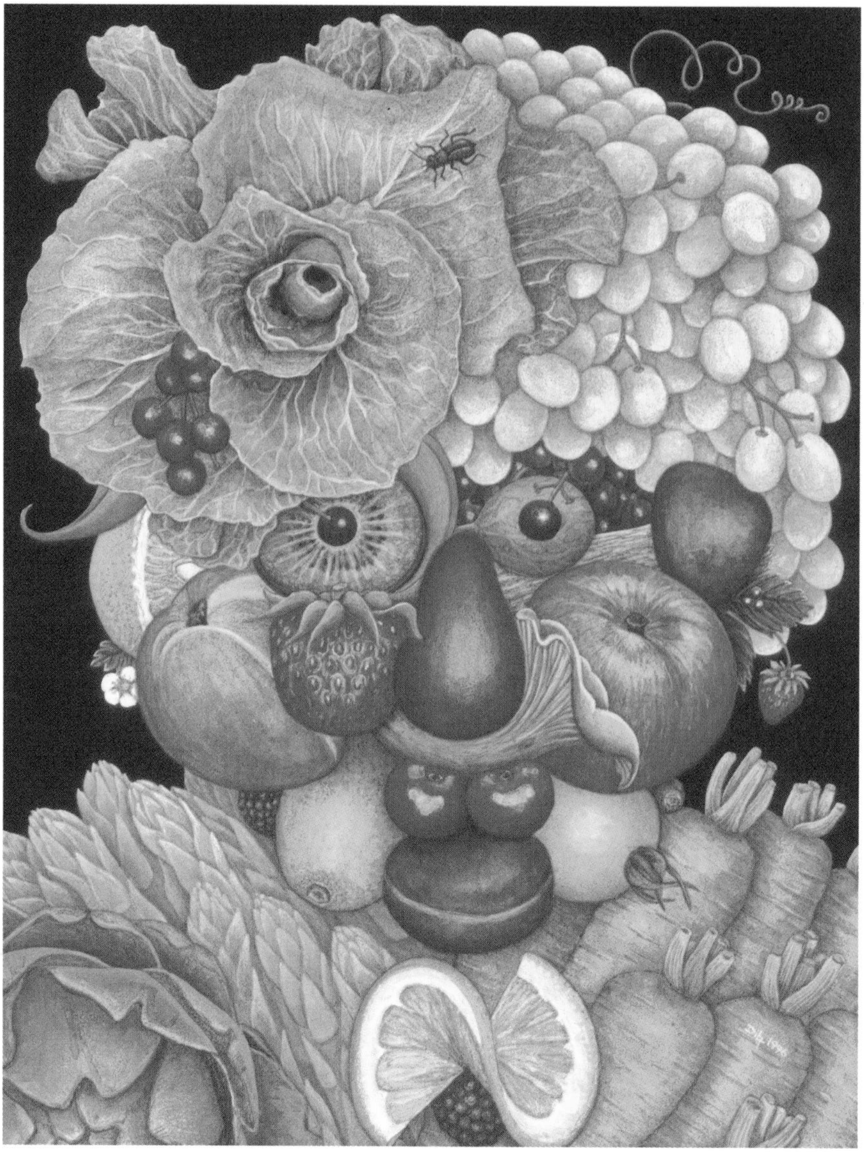

"...she had removed a piece of asparagus from her right eyebrow..."

right eyebrow, and was negotiating for accommodation on the first train going north.

Arriving in London, her first impulse was to go straight to Lancelot. But a natural feminine curiosity urged her, before doing so, to call upon Bernard Worple and have light thrown on some of the more abstruse passages in the telegram.

Worple, in his capacity of author, may have tended towards obscurity, but, when confining himself to the spoken word, he told a plain story well and clearly. Five minutes of his society enabled Gladys to obtain a firm grasp on the salient facts, and there appeared on her face that grim, tight-lipped expression which is seen only on the faces of fiancées who have come back from a short holiday to discover that their dear one has been straying in their absence from the straight and narrow path.

"Brenda Carberry-Pirbright, eh?" said Gladys, with ominous calm. "I'll give him Brenda Carberry-Pirbright! My gosh, if one can't go off to Antibes for the merest breather without one's betrothed getting it up his nose and starting to act like a Mormon Elder, it begins to look a pretty tough world for a girl."

Kind-hearted Bernard Worple did his best.

"I blame the cat," he said. "Lancelot, to my mind, is more sinned against than sinning. I consider him to be acting under undue influence or duress."

"How like a man!" said Gladys. "Shoving it all off onto an innocent cat!"

"Lancelot says it has a sort of something in its eye."

"Well, when I meet Lancelot," said Gladys, "he'll find I have a sort of something in my eye."

She went out, breathing flame quietly through her nostrils. Worple, saddened, heaved a sigh and resumed his neo-Vorticist sculpting.

It was some five minutes later that Gladys, passing through Maxton Square on her way to Bott Street, stopped suddenly in her tracks. The sight she had seen was enough to make any fiancée do so.

Along the pavement leading to No. 11 two figures were advancing. Or three, if you counted a morose-looking dog of a semi-dachshund nature which preceded them, attached to a leash. One of the figures was that of Lancelot Mulliner, natty in grey herringbone tweed and a new Homburg hat. It was he who held the leash. The other Gladys recognized from the portrait she had seen on Lancelot's easel as that modern Du Barry, that notorious wrecker of homes and breaker-up of love-nests, Brenda Carberry-Pirbright.

The next moment they had mounted the steps of No. 11, and had gone into tea, possibly with a little music.

It was perhaps an hour and a half later that Lancelot, having wrenched himself with difficulty from the lair of the Philistines, sped homeward in a taxi. As always after an extended tête-à-tête with Miss Carberry-Pirbright, he felt dazed and bewildered, as if he had been swimming in a sea of glue and had swallowed a great deal of it. All he could think of clearly was that he wanted a drink and that the materials for the drink were in the cupboard behind the Chesterfield of his studio.

He paid the cab and charged in with his tongue rattling dryly against his front teeth. And there before him was Gladys Bingley, whom he had supposed far, far away.

"You!" exclaimed Lancelot.

"Yes, me!" said Gladys.

Her long vigil had not helped to restore the girl's equanimity. Since arriving at the studio she had had the leisure to tap her foot three thousand, one hundred and forty two times on the carpet, and the number of bitter smiles which had flitted across her face was nine hundred and eleven. She was about ready for the battle of the century.

She rose and faced him, all the woman in her flashing from her eyes.

"Well, you Casanova!" she said.

"You who?" said Lancelot.

"Don't you say 'yoo-hoo!' to me!" cried Gladys. "Keep that for your Brenda Carberry-Pirbright. Yes, I know all about it, Lancelot Don Juan Henry the Eighth Mulliner! I saw you with her just now. I hear that you and she are inseparable. Bernard Worple says you said you were going to marry her."

"You mustn't believe everything a neo-Vorticist sculptor tells you," quavered Lancelot.

"I'll bet you're going back to dinner there tonight," said Gladys.

She had spoken at a venture, basing the chance purely on a possessive cock of the head which she had noticed in Brenda Carberry-Pirbright at their recent encounter. There, she had said to herself at the time, had gone a girl who was about to invite – or had just invited - Lancelot Mulliner to dine quietly and take her to the pictures afterwards. But the shot went home. Lancelot hung his head.

"There was some talk of it," he admitted.

"Ah!" exclaimed Gladys.

Lancelot's eyes were haggard.

"I don't want to go," he pleaded. "Honestly, I don't. But Webster insists."

"Webster!"

"Yes, Webster. If I attempt to evade the appointment he'll sit in front of me and look at me."

"Tchah!"

"Well, he will. Ask him for yourself."

Gladys tapped her foot six times in rapid succession on the carpet, bringing the total to three thousand, one hundred and forty eight. Her manner had changed and was now dangerously calm.

"Lancelot Mulliner," she said, "you have your choice. Me, on the one hand, Brenda Carberry-Pirbright on the other. I offer you a home where you will be able to smoke in bed, spill the ashes on the floor, wear pyjamas and carpet slippers all day and shave only on Sunday mornings. From her, what do you have to hope? A house in South Kensington – possibly the Brompton Road – probably with her mother living with you. A life that will be one long round of stiff collars and tight shoes, of morning coats and top hats."

Lancelot quivered, but she went on remorselessly.

"You will be at home on alternate Thursdays, and will be expected to hand out the cucumber sandwiches. Every day you will air the dog, till you become a confirmed dog-airer. You will dine out in Bayswater and go for the summer to Bournemouth or Dinard. Choose well, Lancelot Mulliner! I will leave you to think it over. But one last word. If by seven-thirty on the dot you have not presented yourself at 6a Garbidge Mews ready to take me out to dinner at the Ham and Beef, I shall know what to think and shall act accordingly."

And brushing the cigarette ashes from her chin, the girl strode from the room.

"Gladys!" cried Lancelot.

But she had gone.

For some minutes Lancelot Mulliner remained where he was, stunned. Then, insistently, there came to him the recollection that he had not had that drink. He rushed to the cupboard and produced the bottle. He uncorked it, and was pouring out a lavish stream, when a movement below attracted his attention.

Webster was standing there, looking up at him. And in his eyes was that familiar expression of quiet rebuke.

"Scarcely what I have been accustomed to at the Deanery," he seemed to be saying.

Lancelot stood paralysed. The feeling of being bound hand and foot, of being caught in a snare from which there was no escape, had become more poignant than ever. The bottle fell from his nerveless fingers and rolled across the floor, spilling its contents in an amber river, but he was too heavy in spirit to notice it. With a gesture such as Job might have made on discovering a new boil, he crossed to the window and stood looking moodily out.

Then, turning with a sigh, he looked at Webster again – and, looking, stood spellbound.

The spectacle which he beheld was a kind to stun a stronger man than Lancelot Mulliner. At first, he shrank from believing his eyes. Then, slowly, came the realization that what he saw was no mere figment of a disordered imagination. This unbelievable thing was actually happening.

Webster sat crouched upon the floor beside the widening pool of whisky. But it was not disgust and horror that had caused him to crouch. He was crouched because, crouching, he could get nearer to the stuff and obtain crisper action. His tongue was moving in and out like a piston.

And then abruptly, for one fleeting instant, he stopped lapping and glanced up at Lancelot, and across his face there flitted a quick smile – so genial, so intimate, so full of jovial camaraderie, that the young man found himself automatically smiling back, and not only smiling but winking. And in answer to that wink Webster winked too – a whole-hearted, roguish wink that said as plainly as if he had spoken the words:

"How long has this been going on?"

Then with a slight hiccough he turned back to the task of getting his drink before it soaked into the floor.

Into the murky soul of Lancelot Mulliner there poured a sudden flood of sunshine. It was as if a great burden had been lifted from his shoulders. The intolerable obsession of the last two weeks had ceased to oppress him, and he felt a free man. At the eleventh hour the reprieve had come. Webster, that seeming picture of austere virtue, was one of the boys, after all. Never again would Lancelot quail beneath his eye. He had the goods on him.

Webster, like the stag at eve, had now drunk his fill. He had left the pool of alcohol and was now walking round in slow, meditative circles. From time to time he mewed tentatively, as if he were trying to say 'British Constitution'. His failure to articulate the syllables appeared to tickle him, for at the end of each attempt he would utter a slow, amused chuckle. It was about this moment that he suddenly broke into a rhythmic dance, not unlike the old Saraband.

It was an interesting spectacle, and at any other time Lancelot would have watched it raptly. But now he was busy at his desk, writing a brief note to Mrs Carberry-Pirbright, the burden of which was that if she thought he was coming within a mile of her foul house that night or any other night she had vastly underrated the dodging powers of Lancelot Mulliner.

And what of Webster? The Demon Rum now had him in an iron grip. A lifetime of abstinence had rendered him a ready victim to the fatal fluid. He had now reached the stage when geniality gives way to belligerence. The rather foolish smile had gone from his face, and in its stead there lowered a fighting frown. For a few moments he stood on his hind legs, looking about him for a suitable adversary: then losing all self-control, he ran five times round the room at a high rate of speed and, falling foul of a small footstool, attacked it with the utmost ferocity, sparing neither tooth nor claw.

But Lancelot did not see him. Lancelot was not there. Lancelot was out in Bott Street, hailing a cab.

"6a Garbidge Mews, Fulham," said Lancelot to the driver.

"...a suitable adversary..."

Why?

CHRISTOPHER GUY

"Why do kittens grow into cats?"

Why do kittens grow into cats?
I never saw the sense in that.
I always felt they should stay small
Because I like them that way.
That's all.

The Cat Horoscope

MICHAELA FRIEDERIKE

"...careful about his friends."

VIRGO (August 23 - September 23)

Calculating, calm, self-possessed and careful about his friends. Once he's accepted you he's steadfastly loyal in his quiet undemonstrative way. If you leave your clothes on the bedroom floor he's more likely to walk round them silently showing his disapproval than to curl up purring on top of them.

Best Owners: Capricorn (equally serious and calm and calculating enough to stay one step ahead), Taurus (won't let himself feel under this cat's thumb).
Famous Virgos: Sean Connery, Greta Garbo, Buddy Holly, D.H.Lawrence, Peter Sellers, Bruce Springsteen, Mother Theresa, Leo Tolstoy, H.G.Wells.

Cats At Sea

HENRY FIELDING

Thursday, July 11th, 1754

A most tragical incident fell out this day at sea. While the ship was under sail, but making as would appear no great way, a kitten, one of four of the feline inhabitants of the cabin, fell from the window into the water: an alarm was immediately given to the captain, who was then upon deck, and received it with the utmost concern and many bitter oaths. He immediately gave orders to the steersman in favour of the poor thing, as he called it; the sails were instantly slackened, and all hands, as the phrase is, employed to recover the poor animal. I was, I own, extremely surprised at all this; less indeed at the captain's extreme tenderness than at his conceiving any possibility of success; for if puss had nine thousand instead of nine lives, I concluded they had all been lost. The boatswain, however, had more sanguine hopes, for having stripped himself of his jacket, breeches and shirt, he leapt boldly into the water, and to my great astonishment, in a few minutes returned to the ship, bearing the motionless animal in his mouth. Nor was this, I observed, a matter of such great difficulty as it appeared to my ignorance, and possibly may seem to that of my fresh-water reader. The kitten was now exposed to air and sun on the deck, where its life, of which it retained no symptoms, was despaired by all.

The captain's humanity, if I may so call it, did not so totally destroy his philosophy as to make him yield himself up to affliction on this melancholy occasion. Having felt his loss like a man, he resolved to shew he could bear

"...a kitten, one of four..."

it like one; and having declared he would rather have lost a cask of rum or brandy, betook himself to threshing at backgammon with the Portuguese friar, in which innocent amusement they passed about two-thirds of their time.

But I have, perhaps, a little too wantonly endeavoured to raise the tender passions of my reader in this narrative, I should think myself unpardonable if I concluded it without giving them the satisfaction of hearing that the kitten at last recovered, to the great joy of the good captain, but to the great disappointment of some of the sailors, who asserted that the drowning cat was the very surest way of raising a favourable wind; a supposition of which, though we have heard several plausible accounts, we will not presume to assign the true original reason.

Terry

ALBERT ROWE

terry
my tabby-cat
daylong during winter
tattered ears hugged flat
creeps his wily head
closer and closer
to the heaped coal fire
till the flames
singe his fur
bake his belly

later
after I've appealed
to him vainly
to move when I want
to mend the fire
ignoring the names
I call him will yield
like a blob of mercury
to my touch confident
I'll let him lie I'd rather
let the fire out

when each day
he steps out-
of-doors a bit longer
I know
spring is truly on her way
and when he quits
the house altogether
and sits
trimming and combing his
burnt beard I know
spring has arrived at last

the sun high
he goes to bask
on his back on the path
legs straight and wide
as if tied
bared claws curved to draw
the mouse-warm heat inside
till he begins to purr
and then snore

"biting off heads of flowers"

off heads of flowers
never dead ones
always the brightest ones

nap over

rises

lowers his head

stretches   he swaggers as he walks

heaps his lean belly   pleased I'm watching

high on his back   pleased I'm shaking

becomes for a moment   my rueful head

dromedary

slackens back to cat   stalks slowly to the lilac tree

grins   sits tall egyptian

licks his chops   tigered in leaf light

flirts   yearns for the moment when

a defiant tail   young birds try their flight

deliberately skirts   and flutter from the bough

the border biting   to where he waits below

The Piebald Devil

SVEND FLEURON

One afternoon very early in spring a small, snow-white he-cat came strolling carelessly along the road. His ears were thrust forward, betraying his interest in something ahead: he meant to take a walk round the farm, whither the road led...there was a grey puss there who attracted him!

"...there was a a grey puss there..."

He ought to have been cautious, the little white dwarf! A giant cat, a coloured rival, with the demon of passion seething in his blood and hate flaming from his eyes, caught sight of the hare-brained fellow from afar off and straight-way guessed his errand.

With rigid legs, lowered head and loins held high, he comes rushing from behind...runs noiselessly over the soft grass at the side of the road and overhauls the other unperceived.

With one spring he plants all his foreclaws deep in the flesh of the smaller cat, who utters a loud wail and collapses on the ground.

The big one maintains his grip on the defeated foe's shoulder crushing him ruthlessly in the dust. Then he presses back his torn ears, giving an even more hateful expression to the evil eyes, and lowering his muzzle, gloatingly he howls his song of victory straight into his fallen rival's face.

For a good quarter of an hour he continues to martyr his victim, who is too terrified to move a muscle; he tears the last shred of self-respect and honour from the coward – then releases him and stalks before him to the farm, without deigning to throw him another glance. He was too despicable a rival, the little white mongrel! The big, spotted he-cat considered it beneath his dignity even to thrash him.

But the little grey puss had other suitors still....There was the squire's ginger cat and the bailiff's wicked old black one; so that both daring and cunning were necessary if one's courtship was to be a success. At sunset they invaded the farm from every direction, stealing silently through corn or kitchen garden until they reached the garden path by the hedge.

The black ruffian, who considered himself the favourite suitor, arrived, as he imagined, first at the rendezvous. But simultaneously his ginger rival stuck his head through the hedge bordering the path. At the sight of each other both halted abruptly, thrusting up their backs and blowing out their scarred, battle-torn cheeks.

For many minutes the two ugly fellows stood glaring silently at one another....Then their whiskers bristled, their tattered heads disappeared and their eyes became mere slits in their heads; hymns of hate wailed from their throats, and their tails writhed and squirmed like newly-flayed eels.

Suddenly the big, spotted cat appears in the garden. Tiger-like, with body almost brushing the ground, he glides silently past them.

They hate him, the low brute!...He is their common enemy! The sight of him caught in the act makes them allies in a flash....They tear after him and surround him. They go for him tooth and nail.

All thoughts of the fair one have gone from their minds. War-cries cease; gasps and grunts of exertion punctuate the struggle; chests heave and ribs dilate with compressed air; whilst naked claws are plunged into skin and flesh. They are one to look at, one circular mass, as they whirl round inextricably interlocked, puffing their reeking breaths into one another's faces. The spotted devil's powerful hind legs are wedged in under the red cat's body. With his forepaws he grips him as if in a vice – and now thrusting the needle-pointed, razor-sharp horn daggers from their sheaths, he straightens his hind legs simultaneously to a terrible, resistless, lacerating lunge...

With a stifled hiss of fury the squire's cat falls back. It limps moaning from the battlefield, with blood pouring from its stomach.

Now comes the old black thief's turn! First the hair flies...it literally *steams* from the two rivals as they rush at each other. Their incredible activity is expressed in every movement....After lying interlocked for some time on the ground they suddenly break away, and, as if by witchcraft, stand on all fours again.

The piebald is winning!

His claws comb like steel rakes. They tear the hair from the bailiff-cat's flanks, leaving them bare and shining. The latter often succeeds in parrying, and returns kick for kick, but his hind legs lack strength and he cannot complete a full thrust.

Madness gleams in their eyes; they are beside themselves with frenzy;

"There was the squire's ginger cat..."

fear flies from their minds; they are exalted…for now they are *fighting!*

Until a sudden scuffle advertises that the bailiff-cat has had enough. He tears himself loose and bolts for his life.

The big piebald has won. He shakes himself and rolls over, gives a couple of energetic licks to his paws, and carefully brushes his whiskers; then he hastens through the garden to the farmyard, where a little while later is to be seen promenading on the pigsty roof.

With an alert expression and nervously vibrating tail he looks enquiringly at all trap-doors and open windows. Suddenly he gives a start;

"He was all possible colours – black, red, yellow, and white."

there is Grey Puss on the manure heap beneath him. Without a moment's hesitation he leaps down....It was the decisive meeting!

She has always been true to this one lover....And yet there had been times when all the gentlemen of the neighbourhood had paid court to her. Often she had reclined on the planking with one in front of her, one behind, and three or four in the elder tree above her head....She had been literally besieged.

But however many suitors might appear – even though they came right up from the seacoast and the fishing village – she still loved him and him alone, the great piebald hero!

He was an exceptional cat; the ears, far apart and noticeably short, were set far back on the broad head; the neck was thick and powerful, the body long and heavy. When he ran he moved with such swiftness that he seemed to glide, and could leap two yards without effort.

He was all possible colours – black, red, yellow, and white. A tinge of green shone in the wicked golden eyes; they sat deep in his head, so that his cheeks stuck out on each side like dumplings....And in the middle of his bristly moustache protruded a small lacerated nose, which was always bright red and covered with half-healed wounds. He was always at war....

Once he received a deep, horrid bite just under the throat, where he could not lick it. So he went to his sweetheart; she helped him....

She was faithful and true to him...but she did not trust him beyond the threshold.

Had she reason to doubt him? He was chock full of lust and vice, and great in merit as in fault; nevertheless – had she actual proof for doubting him? One night her eyes were opened in the most sinister manner. The last rays of the setting sun had departed from the fields, leaving them wrapped in the summer evening's mist and obscurity. Only some horses greeted the solitary marauder with warm, friendly neighing.

They knew him well, although he was only a cat, whose many coloured body seemed grey, like all other cats, in the twilight. In the doorway, at the pump, in yard and stable he was their daily companion. How nice to see him here on the meadow too! "Ehehehe," they neighed…welcome to the tethering ground!

He ignored them completely, neither breaking his stride, nor wagging his tail, nor giving a single miauw. Past nuisances like foals which greeted him boisterously he went unresponsive and bored. He was out hunting now – nothing else mattered.

With gliding step he passes from clover field to seed ground, jumping with noiseless, tense spring over brook and ditch. His progress roused the lark from heavy slumber.

He reaches a copse – and soon afterward is heard the death-shriek of a captured blackbird. With covetous grasp he seizes his victim, buries his sharp teeth in its breast, and sucks with long sniffs the warm, odorous bird-smell….

It was not hunger which drove him to the crime: he has just made a full meal off a couple of fat mice. But when coming unexpectedly upon the bird in the copse, he could not control his murderous impulse.

He sits with the booty in his jaws, purring contentedly, and ponders frowningly where he shall conceal his capture.

The summer moon shines big and round from the pale blue, starless sky – and white, pink-underlined layers of cloud hover like feathers far out on the horizon. Warm puffs of wind come and go, enveloping him in the meadow's silver mist, making the dim shelter of the hedge seem hot and oppressive.

His eyes fall on the three ancient willow stumps at the far end of the field! He, too, knows how rotten and hollow they are, and how well adapted for a hiding place. True, it is rather a long way there…through the soaking wet rye – but that can't be helped!

The night is absolutely silent, broken only by the rasping song of the little reed-warbler from a swampy hole among the rye. The din of the farm has long since died down; not even the bark of a dog is heard, and neither water-pump nor wind-motor can summon up another note. How splendid to have ears, to be able to listen! Now he hears only the play of the grasshoppers, the love-song of the cockchafer and the high-pitched music of the anthills.

Here, behind a knotted root at the base of the largest of the old willow trees, he conceals the blackbird, afterwards covering it carefully with earth and moss. Then he reaches his forepaws up to the trunk to stretch his limbs and sharpen his claws.

He gives a violent start! The scarred, rugged skin on his head wrinkles thoughtfully, as it always does when something attracts his attention. His multicoloured tail jerks uneasily, as he peers about him with uplifted ears.

The subdued rustling and squeaking noises from inside the tree trunk continue….

Now there is no longer room for doubt….

With a giant leap he springs up the tree, and next moment he is in the bole. Grey Puss is not at home….

The little kittens swarm up to him. Tiny seeks to drink, while Black and Big make a joyful assault on his swiftly wagging tail. He lowers his nose to each of the little fellows in turn as if tasting their smell. Then, as if he has gone mad, he begins clawing about in all directions at the defenceless kittens.

Mewing and squealing, they roll away to all sides like lumps of earth – but the he-cat's frenzy increases.

He seizes Tiny by the mouth, fixes an eye tooth in his scruff and hurtles out of the willow with him. The little tot hangs limp and apparently lifeless in the jaw of his brutal sire; but, fortunately for him the old cat is not hungry, and so is content with burying the kitten at the foot of the willow, by the side of the dead blackbird.

In justice to the criminal it must be stated that he has no conception of the enormity of his crime; only when he is on his way up the willow for the second time is he enlightened – and that in a most ruthless manner. Two rows of gimlet-pointed claws descend from nowhere and almost nail him to the bark….Furious, he turns his visage…and the next second all his old half-healed wounds are torn open again!

Grey Puss has surprised him – and recognises him instantly. So it is he who comes wrecking her maternal happiness; yes, she thought as much! And like a vice she clings to his back, biting and scratching and tearing as he flees panic-stricken along the hedge.

Away, away, home, anywhere!

He is more afraid of Grey Puss' mother-claws than of the raven's beak or the blade of the reaping-machine; he has learnt to his cost that a she-cat knows not the word mercy when her swollen udders are carrying milk for her young.

He lacked a conscience, this big, piebald he-cat – and he respected nothing except his own skin! The egg of the lark, the chick of the partridge, the young of the hare, were each grist to his mill; he took everything he could find, catch, or steal. On the rafter at home in the farmyard, where Grey Puss used to lie, he had been allowed free passage, until the very moment when

"Ehehehe, they neighed...welcome..."

some small bundles lay shivering on the hay in the corner. Then the fascination of his black face and shining coat seemed to vanish; she would not allow him to approach; he was not even admitted to the barn. If he just showed himself at the trap-door she would become seized with frenzy, spring up and fly at him as if he were a dog! He had always to beat a hurried retreat!

Did she read his character; did she know that the feeling of paternal love was foreign to his nature? In any case, she took no risks; she never trusted him over the threshold....

Grey Puss' milk tasted sour for a whole day following the adventure; she was frightfully restless and upset. Several of the young had wounds and had to be licked. Time after time she ran her glance over the small, rolled up batches of colour; greedily her eyes devoured each little furry coat; but it was with no trace of the sweetness of recollection or the joy of recognition.

Were they all there...all? Their villain of a father she had already forgotten; not until she was giving suck did she become suddenly nervous. She felt now that one of the swollen udders remained swollen, and now she nuzzled with her nose along the row. Big, Red, White ,Grey...yes, she found them all! But where was the little piebald one?

The kittens buried their noses deep in her fur to get a good hold of the small, sprouting milk-springs. All was quiet inside the willow trunk; only now and again was heard the sucking of eager little lips....

Yes, to be sure, she missed a colour...missed just that one which – in spite of all – she unconsciously preferred to all the rest; that seemed to be made up of bits of colour from all the other colours....Then suddenly a thin, feeble crying reached her ever-listening ears. It seemed to her to come from under the willow bole. Perhaps there was a crevice in the nursery?

Cautiously getting up, she begins to scratch a little with her forepaws in the floor; but finds no hole.

She dismisses the thought that one of the young ones is really missing, and lies down again and resumes her maternal duties. For a time all is peace, and she abandons herself completely to the pleasure of being at the mercy of her kitten-flock, but again comes the faint cry for help. This time it is so heart-rending that she springs up, and then, half crouching, listens breathlessly.

"Mew, mew!" it tinkles to her from the distant depths. And now she begins to answer in anxious, encouraging tones, meanwhile pushing her snout among the young ones to count them. The tinkling from below upsets and worries her; but presently she stifles her anxiety by rolling right under the heap of kittens and congratulating herself that she has so many dear children safe and sound.

Meanwhile from his living tomb by the side of the blackbird, Tiny continues foghornlike, to emit at regular intervals his ceaseless signals for assistance. He has lain a long time buried alive; but, accustomed as he is to having brothers and sisters on top of him, the thin layer of moss and earth over him does not embarrass him particularly. Now he has recovered so much that he can not only squeal but wriggle also – a fact which serves to increase the air supply in his lungs, so that his weak cries gain momentarily in strength and resonance.

Suddenly the heap of earth is swept from him, and he hears his mother's soft voice right in his ear. Oh, what a stream of happiness flows through him! He stretches his tiny body towards the strong comforting miauw, and like a freezing man makes for the fire, he puts his wet, earth-cold head against the mother-cat's soft neck and feels her warm breath ripple over him.

Grey Puss' eyes shine green and evil; they speak plainly of surprise and emotion. She begins purring angrily, so that the young ones in the tree lift their ears anxiously and wonder. "What's happening down there at the foot of the tree?"

Tiny's wound is licked, and the mother prepares to return. He must be carried, of course…and the problem is to find a hold which will not destroy the creature. She tries to grasp him by the scruff, but here he is so sore that time after time the attempt fails. Cautiously she presses her teeth into his back and shoulder; but cannot find a hold, although he seeks instinctively to help her by stiffening his body as she lifts.

However, it must be done somehow; there is not the slightest doubt that he is to be carried up! So she opens her mouth wide and puts her jaws round his neck. Then, disregarding his lively protests, she cautiously closes her mouth.

He becomes suddenly quite quiet. She needs all her presence of mind to judge how tightly she may grip him without making it his last journey.

He hangs there in his mother's jaws and closes his earth-logged eyes, clutching her body tightly with his little legs. But he surrenders himself to her without complaint and without movement, bearing the pain in blind faith in her omnipotence.

In two jumps she reaches the top, slides down into the bole, and a moment later deposits him carefully on the ground among the others. A healing warmth envelops him – and, as the kittens are already satisfied, he secures an unusually large share of milk.

The Cat Horoscope

MICHAELA FRIEDERIKE

"…the comfort of your lap."

LIBRA (September 24 - October 23)

Hates to be impolite but can't control the need to control…If he was human he'd straighten up the pictures hanging on the wall in someone else's house. He's content quietly and carefully to rearrange the world from the comfort of your lap. He prefers a one-to-one relationship and is not happy in crowds.

Best Owners: Gemini (his outgoing nature can sometimes, but not always, be a good foil to the Libran's introversion) Leo (dominant, a natural leader).
Famous Librans: Brigitte Bardot, Sarah Bernhardt, Truman Capote, T.S. Eliot, George Gershwin, John Lennon, Cliff Richard, Verdi, Oscar Wilde.

Country Cat

ELIZABETH COATSWORTH

"Where are you going, Mrs. Cat,
All by your lonesome lone?"
"Hunting a mouse, or maybe a rat
Where the ditches are overgrown."

"But you're very far from your house and home,
You've come a long, long way-"
"The further I wander, the longer I roam
The more I find mice at play."

"But you're very near to the dark pinewood
And foxes go hunting too."
"I know that a fox might find me good,
But what is a cat to do?"

"I have my kittens who must be fed,
I can't have them skin and bone!"
And Mrs. Cat shook her brindled head
And went off by her lonesome lone.

"I know that a fox might find me good…"

Tobermory

SAKI

It was a chill, rain-washed afternoon of a late August day, that indefinite season when partridges are still in the security of cold storage, and there is nothing to hunt – unless one is bounded on the north by the Bristol Channel, in which case one may lawfully gallop after fat red stags. Lady Blemley's house-party was not bounded on the north by the Bristol Channel, hence there was a full gathering of her guests round the tea-table this particular afternoon. And, in spite of the blankness of the season and the triteness of the occasion, there was no trace in the company of that fatigued restlessness which means a dread of the pianola and a subdued hankering for auction bridge. The undisguised open-mouthed attention of the entire party was fixed on the homely, negative personality of Mr Cornelius Appin. Of all her guests, he was the one who had come to Lady Blemley with the vaguest reputation. Someone had said he was 'clever', and he had got his invitation in the moderate expectation, on the part of his hostess, that some portion at least of his cleverness would be contributed to the general entertainment. Until tea-time that day she had been unable to discover in what direction, if any, his cleverness lay. He was neither a wit nor a croquet champion, a hypnotic force nor a begetter of amateur theatricals. Neither did his exterior suggest the type of man in whom women are willing to pardon a generous measure of mental deficiency. He had subsided into mere Mr Appin, and the Cornelius part seemed a piece of transparent baptismal bluff. And now he was claiming to have launched on the world a discovery beside which the

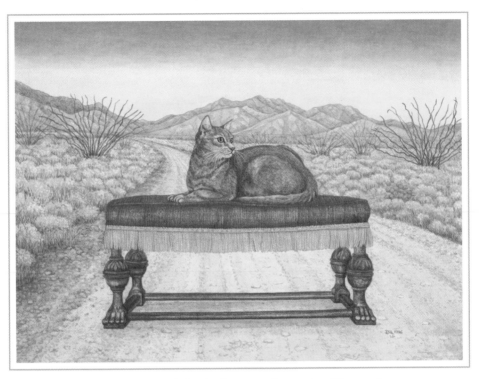

"...a 'Beyond-Cat' of extraordinary intelligence."

invention of gun powder, of the printing-press, and of steam locomotion were inconsiderable trifles. Science had made bewildering strides in many directions during recent decades, but this thing seemed to belong to the domain of miracle rather than to scientific achievement.

"And do you really ask us to believe," Sir Wilfred was saying, "that you have discovered a means for instructing animals in the art of human speech, and that dear old Tobermory has proved your first successful pupil?"

"It is a problem at which I have worked for the last seventeen years," said Mr Appin, "but only during the last eight or nine months have I been

"I found him in the smoking room…"

rewarded with a glimmering of success. Of course I have experimented with thousands of animals, but latterly only with cats, those wonderful creatures which have assimilated themselves so marvelously with our civilization while retaining all their highly developed feral instincts.

Here and there among cats one comes across an outstanding superior intellect, just as one does among the ruck of human beings, and when I made the acquaintance of Tobermory a week ago I saw at once that I was in contact with a 'Beyond-Cat' of extraordinary intelligence. I had gone far along the road to success in recent experiments; with Tobermory, as you call him, I have reached the goal."

Mr Appin concluded his remarkable statement in a voice which he strove to divest of a triumphant inflexion. No one said 'Rats', though Clovis' lips moved in a monosyllabic contortion which probably invoked those rodents of disbelief.

"And do you mean to say," asked Miss Resker, after a slight pause, "that you have taught Tobermory to say and understand sentences of one syllable?"

"My dear Miss Resker," said the wonder-worker patiently, "one teaches little children and savages and backward adults in that piecemeal fashion; when one has solved the problem of making a beginning with an animal of highly developed intelligence one has no need for those halting methods. Tobermory can speak our language with perfect correctness."

This time Clovis very distinctly said "Beyond-Rats!" Sir Wilfred was more polite, but equally skeptical.

"Hadn't we better have the cat in and judge for ourselves?" suggested Lady Blemley.

Sir Wilfred went in search of the animal, and the company settled themselves down to the languid expectation of witnessing some more or less adroit ventriloquism.

In a minute Sir Wilfred was back in the room, his face white beneath its tan and his eyes dilated with excitement.

"By Gad, it's true!"

His agitation was unmistakably genuine, and his hearers started forward in a thrill of awakened interest.

Collapsing into an armchair he continued breathlessly, "I found him dozing in the smoking room, and called after him to come for his tea. He blinked at me in his usual way, and I said, 'Come on, Toby; don't keep us waiting!' and, by Gad! He drawled out in a most horribly natural voice, that he'd come when he dashed well pleased! I nearly jumped out of my skin!"

Appin had preached to absolutely incredulous hearers; Sir Wilfred's statement carried instant conviction. A Babel-like chorus of startled exclamation arose, amid which the scientist sat mutely enjoying the first fruit of his stupendous discovery.

In the midst of the clamour Tobermory entered the room and made his way with velvet tread and studied unconcern across to the group seated around the tea-table.

A sudden hush of awkwardness and constraint fell on the company. Somehow there seemed an element of embarrassment in addressing on equal terms a domestic cat of acknowledged mental ability.

"Will you have some milk Tobermory?" asked Lady Blemley in a rather strained voice.

"I don't mind if I do," was the response, couched in a tone of even indifference. A shiver of suppressed excitement went through the listeners, and Lady Blemley might be excused for pouring out the saucerful of milk rather unsteadily.

"I am afraid I have spilled a good deal of it," she said apologetically.

"After all, it's not my Axminster," was Tobermory's rejoinder.

Another silence fell on the group, and then Miss Resker, in her best district-visitor manner, asked if the human language had been difficult to learn. Tobermory looked squarely at her for a moment and then fixed his gaze serenely on the middle distance. It was obvious that boring questions lay outside his scheme of life.

"What do you think of human intelligence?" asked Mavis Pellington lamely.

"Of whose intelligence in particular?" asked Tobermory coldly.

"Oh, well, mine for instance," said Mavis, with a feeble laugh.

"You put me in an embarrassing position," said Tobermory, whose tone and attitude certainly did not suggest a shred of embarrassment. "When your inclusion in this house party was suggested, Sir Wilfred protested that you were the most brainless woman of his acquaintance, and that there was a wide distinction between hospitality and care of the feeble-minded. Lady Blemley replied that your lack of brain-power was the precise quality which had earned your invitation, as you were the only person she could think of who might be idiotic enough to buy their old car. You know, the one they call 'The Envy of Sisyphus', because it goes quite nicely uphill if you push it."

Lady Blemley's protestations would have had greater effect if she had not casually mentioned to Mavis only that morning that the car in question would be just the thing for her down at her Devonshire home.

Major Barfield plunged in heavily to effect a diversion.

"How about your carryings-on with the tortoiseshell puss up at the stables, eh?"

The moment he had said it everyone realized the blunder.

"One does not usually discuss these matters in public," said Tobermory frigidly. "From a slight observation of your ways since you've been in this house I should imagine you'd find it inconvenient if I were to shift the conversation on to your own little affairs."

The panic which ensued was not confined to the Major.

"Would you like to go and see if cook has got your dinner ready?" suggested Lady Blemley hurriedly, affecting to ignore the fact that it wanted at least two hours to Tobermory's dinner-time.

"Thanks," said Tobermory, "not quite so soon after my tea. I don't want to die of indigestion."

"Cats have nine lives, you know," said Sir Wilfred heartily.

"...the big yellow Tom from the Rectory..."

"Possibly," answered Tobermory; "but only one liver."

"Adelaide!" said Mrs Cornett, "do you mean to encourage that cat to go out and gossip about us in the servant's hall?"

The panic had indeed become general. A narrow ornamental balustrade ran in front of most of the bedrooms at the Towers, and it was recalled with dismay that this had formed a favourite promenade for Tobermory at all hours, whence he could watch the pigeons – and heaven knew what else besides. If he intended to become reminiscent in his present outspoken strain the effect would be something more than disconcerting. Mrs Cornett, who spent much time at her toilet table, and whose complexion was reputed to be of a nomadic though punctual disposition, looked as ill at ease as the Major. Miss Scrawen, who wrote fiercely sensuous poetry and led a blameless life, merely displayed irritation; if you are methodical and virtuous in private you don't necessarily want everyone to know it. Bertie van Tahn, who was so depraved at seventeen that he had long ago given up trying to be any worse, turned a dull shade of gardenia white, but he did not commit the error of dashing out of the room like Otto Finsbury, a young gentleman who was understood to be reading for the Church and who was possibly disturbed at the thought of the scandals he might hear concerning other people. Clovis had the presence of mind to maintain a composed exterior; privately he was calculating how long it would take to procure a box of fancy mice through the agency of *Exchange and Mart* as a species of hush money.

Even in a delicate situation like the present, Agnes Resker could not endure to remain too long in the background.

"Why did I ever come down here?" she asked dramatically. Tobermory immediately accepted the opening.

"Judging by what you were saying to Mrs Cornett on the croquet lawn yesterday, you were out for food. You described the Blemleys as the dullest people to stay with that you knew, but said they were clever enough to employ a first rate cook; otherwise they'd find it difficult to get anyone to come down a second time."

"There's not a word of truth in it! I appeal to Mrs Cornett –" exclaimed the discomfited Agnes.

"Mrs Cornett repeated your remark afterwards to Bertie van Than," continued Tobermory, and said "That woman is a regular Hunger-Marcher; she'd go anywhere for four square meals a day, and Bertie van Than said –"

At this point the chronicle mercifully ceased. Tobermory had caught a glimpse of the big yellow Tom from the Rectory working his way through the shrubbery towards the stable wing. In a flash he had vanished through the open French window.

With the disappearance of his too brilliant pupil Cornelius Appin found himself beset by a hurricane of bitter upbraiding, anxious enquiry, and frightened entreaty. The responsibility for the situation lay with him, and he must prevent matters from becoming worse. Could Tobermory impart his dangerous gift to other cats? was the first question he had to answer. It was possible, he replied, that he might have initiated his intimate friend the stable puss into his new accomplishment, but it was unlikely that his teaching could have taken a wider range as yet.

"Then," said Mrs Cornett, "Tobermory may be a valuable cat and a great pet; but I'm sure you'll agree, Adelaide, that both he and the stable cat must be done away with without delay."

"You don't suppose I've enjoyed the last quarter of an hour, do you?" said Lady Blemley bitterly. "My husband and I are very fond of Tobermory –

"...his intimate friend the stable puss..."

at least, we were before this horrible accomplishment was infused into him; but now, of course the only thing is to have him destroyed as soon as possible."

"We can put some strychnine in the scraps he always gets at dinnertime," said Sir Wilfred, "and I will go and drown the stable cat myself. The coachman will be very sore at losing his pet, but I'll say a very catching form

"...go and experiment on the short-horns..."

of mange has broken out in both cats and we're afraid of it spreading to the kennels."

"But my great discovery!" expostulated Mr Appin; "after all my years of research and experiment –"

"You can go and experiment on the short-horns at the farm, who are under proper control," said Mrs Cornett, "or the elephants at the Zoological Gardens. They're said to be highly intelligent, and they have this recommendation, that they don't come creeping about our bedrooms and under chairs, and so forth."

An archangel ecstatically proclaiming the Millennium, and then finding that it clashed with Henley and would have to be indefinitely postponed, could hardly have felt more crestfallen than Cornelius Appin at the reception of his wonderful achievements. Public opinion, however, was against him – in fact, had the general voice been consulted on the subject it is probable that a strong minority vote would have been in favour of including him in the strychnine diet.

Defective train arrangements and a nervous desire to see matters brought to a finish prevented an immediate dispersal of the party, but dinner that evening was not a social success. Sir Wilfred had had rather a trying time with the stable cat and subsequently with the coachman. Agnes Resker ostentatiously limited her repast to a morsel of dry toast, which she bit as though it were a personal enemy, while Mavis Pellington maintained a vindictive silence throughout the meal. Lady Blemley kept up a flow of what she hoped was conversation, but her attention was fixed on the doorway. A plateful of carefully dosed fish scraps was in readiness on the sideboard, but sweets and savoury and dessert went their way and no Tobermory appeared either in the dining-room or kitchen.

The sepulchral dinner was cheerful compared with the subsequent vigil in the smoking-room. Eating and drinking had at least supplied a distraction and cloak to the prevailing embarrassment. Bridge was out of the question in the general tension of nerves and tempers, and after Odo Finsberry had given a lugubrious rendering of 'Melisande in the Wood' to a frigid audience, music was tacitly avoided. At eleven the servants went to bed, announcing that the small window in the pantry had been left open as usual for Tobermory's private use. The guests read steadily through the current batch of magazines, and fell back gradually on the 'Badminton Library' and bound volumes of *Punch*. Lady Blemley made periodic visits to the pantry, returning each time with an expression of listless depression which forestalled questioning. At two o'clock Clovis broke the dominating silence.

"He won't turn up tonight. He's probably in the local newspaper office at the present moment, dictating the first instalment of his reminiscences. Lady What's-her-name's book won't be in it. It will be the event of the day."

Having made this contribution to the general cheerfulness, Clovis went to bed. At long intervals the various members of the house party followed his example.

The servants taking round the early tea made a uniform announcement in reply to a uniform question. Tobermory had not returned. Breakfast was, if anything, a more unpleasant function than dinner had been, but before its conclusion the situation was relieved. Tobermory's corpse was brought in from the shrubbery, where a gardener had just discovered it. From the bites on his throat and the yellow fur which coated his claws it was evident that he had fallen in unequal combat with the big Tom from the Rectory.

By midday most of the guests had quitted the Towers, and after lunch Lady Blemley had sufficiently recovered her spirits to write an extremely nasty letter to the Rectory about the loss of her valuable pet.

Tobermory had been Appin's one successful pupil, and he was destined to have no successor. A few weeks later an elephant in the Dresden Zoological Garden, which had shown no previous sign of irritability, broke loose and killed an Englishman who had apparently been teasing it. The victim's name was variously reported as Oppin and Eppelin, but his front name was faithfully rendered Cornelius.

"If he was trying German irregular verbs on the poor beast," said Clovis, "he deserved all he got."

Last Words to a Dumb Friend

THOMAS HARDY

"...plumy tail, and wistful gaze..."

Pet was never mourned as you,
Purrer of the spotless hue,
Plumy tail, and wistful gaze,
While you humoured our queer ways,
Or outshrilled your morning call
Up the stairs and through the hall –
Foot suspended in its fall –
While, expectant, you would stand
Arched, to meet the stroking hand;
Till your way you chose to wend
Yonder, to your tragic end.

Never another pet for me!
Let your place all vacant be;
Better blankness day by day
Than companion torn away.
Better bid his memory fade,
Better blot each mark he made,
Selfishly escape distress
By contrived forgetfulness,
Than preserve his prints to make
Every morn and eve an ache.

From the chair whereon he sat
Sweep his fur, nor wince thereat;
Rake his little pathways out
Mid the bushes roundabout;
Smooth away his talons' mark
From the claw-worn pine-tree bark,
Where he climbed as dusk embrowned
Waiting us who loitered round.

Strange it is this speechless thing,
Subject to our mastering,
Subject for his life and food
To our gift, and time, and mood;
Timid pensioner of us Powers,
His existence ruled by ours,
Should – by crossing at a breath

Into a safe and shielded death,
By the merely taking hence
Of his insignificance –
Loom as largened to the sense,
Shape as part, above man's will,
Of the Imperturbable.

As a prisoner, flight debarred,
Exercising in a yard,
Still retain I, troubled, shaken,
Mean estate, by him forsaken;
And this home, which scarcely took
Impress from his little look,
By his faring to the Dim,
Grows all eloquent of him.

Housemate, I can think you still
Bounding to the window-sill,
Over which I vaguely see
Your small mound beneath the tree,
Showing in the autumn shade
That you moulder where you played.

The Cat Horoscope

MICHAELA FRIEDERIKE

"...you'll never have the nerve to ask him to get off that sofa."

SCORPIO (October 24 - November 22)

Likes to travel incognito; you won't see him coming, unless he wants you to. His hypnotic eyes can persuade you to do anything he demands and demand he will... Sometimes you feel he can read your thoughts. With an overdeveloped sense of his own importance you'll never have the nerve to ask him to get off your favourite chair or that antique sofa.

Best Owners: Pisces (carefree, intuitive, patient, good-natured).
Famous Scorpios: Marie Antoinette, John Cleese, Marie Curie, Bill Gates, Katherine Hepburn, John Keats, Martin Luther, Claude Monet, Picasso.

A Mutual Entertainment

MONTAIGNE

"...my cat and I entertain each other..."

When my cat and I entertain each other with mutual apish tricks, as playing with a garter, who knows but that I make my cat more sport than she makes me? Shall I conclude her to be simple, that has her time to begin or refuse to play as freely as I myself have? Nay, who knows but that it is a defect of my not understanding her language (for doubtless cats talk and reason with one another) that we agree no better? And who knows but that she pities me for being no wiser than to play with her, and laughs and censures my folly for making sport for her, when we two play together?

A Cat

EDWARD THOMAS

She had a name among the children;
But no one loved her though some one owned
Her, locked her out of doors at bedtime,
And had her kittens duly drowned.

In spring, nevertheless, this cat
Ate blackbirds, thrushes, nightingales,
And birds of bright voice, and plume and flight,
As well as scraps from neighbours' pails.

I loathed and hated her for this;
One speckle on a thrush's breast
Was worth a million such; and yet
She lived long till God gave her rest.

"…this cat ate birds of bright voice and plume…"

The Kitten and the Falling-Leaves

WILLIAM WORDSWORTH

"...withered leaves..."

That way look, my Infant, lo!
What a pretty baby show!
See the kitten on the wall,
Sporting with the leaves that fall,
Withered leaves – one – two – and three –
From the lofty elder tree!
Through the calm and frosty air
Of this morning bright and fair,
Eddying round and round they sink
Softly, slowly: one might think,
From the motions that are made,
Every little leaf conveyed
Sylph or Faery hither tending –

To this lower world descending,
Each invisible and mute,
In his wavering parachute.
But the kitten, how she starts,
Crouches, stretches, paws and darts!
First at one, and then its fellow;
Just as light and just as yellow;
There are many now - now one –
Now they stop and then are none:
What intenseness of desire
In her upward eye of fire!
With a tiger-leap half-way
Now she meets the coming prey,
Lets it go as fast, and then
Has it in her power again:
Now she works with three or four,
Like an Indian conjurer;
Quick as he in feats of art,
Far beyond in joy of heart.
Were her antics played in the eye
Of a thousand standers-by,
Clapping hands with shout and stare,
What would little tabby care
For the plaudits of the crowd?
Over happy to be proud,
Over wealthy in the treasure
Of her own exceeding pleasure!...

From

Far from the Madding Crowd

THOMAS HARDY

Nothing disturbed the stillness of the cottage save the chatter of a knot of sparrows on the eaves; one might fancy scandal and rumour to be no less the staple topic of these little coteries on the roofs than of those under them. It seemed the omen was an unpropitious one, for, at the rather untoward commencement of Oak's adventures, just as he arrived by the garden gate he saw a cat inside, going into various arched shapes and fiendish convulsions at the sight of his dog George. The dog took no notice, for he had arrived at an age at which all superfluous barking was cynically avoided as a waste of breath – in fact, he never barked even at the sheep except to order, when it was done with an absolutely neutral countenance, as a sort of Commination – service which, though offensive, had to be gone through once now and then to frighten the flock for their own good.

"...going into various arched shapes at the sight of his dog..."

The Cat

MARY E. WILKINS

The snow was falling, and the Cat's fur was stiffly pointed with it, but he
was imperturbable. He sat crouched, ready for the death-spring, as he had
sat for hours. It was night – but that made no difference – all times were as
one to the Cat when he was in wait for prey. Then, too, he was under no
constraint of human will, for he was living alone that winter. Nowhere in the
world was any voice calling him; on no hearth was there a waiting dish. He
was quite free except for his own desires, which tyrannised over him when
unsatisfied as now. The Cat was very hungry - almost famished, in fact. For
days the weather had been very bitter, and all the feebler wild things which
were his prey by inheritance, the born serfs to his family, had kept, for the
most part, in their burrows and nests, and the Cat's long hunt had availed
him nothing. But he waited with the inconceivable patience and persistency
of his race; besides, he was certain. The Cat was a creature of absolute
convictions, and his faith in his deductions never wavered. The rabbit had
gone in there between those low-hung pine boughs. Now her little doorway
had before it a shaggy curtain of snow, but in there she was. The Cat had
seen her enter, so like a swift gray shadow that even his sharp and practised
eyes had glanced back for the substance following, and then she was gone.
So he sat down and waited, and he waited still in the white night, listening
angrily to the north wind starting in the upper heights of the mountains with

distant screams, then swelling into an awful crescendo of rage, and swooping down with furious white wings of snow like a flock of fierce eagles into the valleys and ravines. The Cat was on the side of a mountain, on a wooded terrace. Above him a few feet away towered the rock ascent as steep as the wall of a cathedral. The Cat had never climbed it – trees were ladders to his heights of life. He often looked with wonder at the rock, and miauled bitterly and resentfully as man does in the face of a forbidding Providence. At his left was the sheer precipice. Behind him, with a short stretch of woody growth between, was the frozen perpendicular fall of a mountain stream. Before him was the way to his home. When the rabbit came out she was trapped; her little cloven feet could not scale such unbroken steeps. So the Cat waited. The place in which he was looked like a maelstrom of the wood. The tangle of trees and bushes clinging to the mountain-side with a stern clutch of roots, the prostrate trunks and branches, the vines embracing everything with strong knots and coils of growth, had a curious effect, as of things whirled for ages in a current of raging water, only it was not water, but wind, which had disposed everything in circling lines of yielding to its fiercest points of onset. And now over all this whirl of wood and rock and dead trunks and branches and vines descended the snow. It blew down like smoke over the rock-crest above; it stood in a gyrating column like some death-wraith of nature, on the level, then it broke over the edge of the precipice, and the Cat cowered before the fierce backward set of it. It was as if ice needles pricked his skin through his beautiful thick fur, but he never faltered and never once cried. He had nothing to gain from crying and everything to lose; the rabbit would hear him cry and know he was waiting.

It grew darker and darker, with a strange white smother, instead of the natural blackness of night. It was a night of storm and death superadded to

"…the rabbit would hear him cry."

the night of nature. The mountains were all hidden, wrapped about, overawed, and tumultuously overborne by it, but in the midst of it waited, quite unconquered, this little, unswerving, living patience and power under a little coat of gray fur.

A fiercer blast swept over the rock, spun on one mighty foot of whirlwind athwart the level, then was over the precipice.

Then the Cat saw two eyes luminous with terror, frantic with the impulse of flight, he saw a little, quivering, dilating nose, he saw two pointing ears, and he kept still, with every one of his fine nerves and muscles strained like wires. Then the rabbit was out – there was one long line of incarnate flight and terror – and the Cat had her.

Then the Cat went home, trailing his prey through the snow.

The Cat lived in the house which his master had built, as rudely as a child's blockhouse, but staunchly enough. The snow was heavy on the low slant of its roof, but it would not settle under it. The two windows and the door were made fast, but the Cat knew a way in. Up a pine-tree behind the house he scuttled, though it was hard work with his heavy rabbit, and was in his little window under the eaves, then down through the trap to the room below, and on his master's bed with a spring and a great cry of triumph, rabbit and all. But his master was not there; he had been gone since early fall, and it was now February. He would not return until spring, for he was an old man, and the cruel cold of the mountains clutched at his vitals like a panther, and he had gone to the village to winter. The Cat had known for a long time that his master was gone, but his reasoning was always sequential and circuitous; always for him what had been would be, and the more easily for his marvellous waiting powers, so he always came home expecting to find his master.

When he saw that he was still gone, he dragged the rabbit off the rude couch which was the bed to the floor, put one paw on the carcass to keep it steady, and began gnawing with head to one side to bring his strongest teeth to bear.

It was darker in the house than it had been in the wood, and the cold was as deadly, though not so fierce. If the Cat had not received his fur coat unquestioningly of Providence, he would have been thankful that he had it. It was a mottled gray, white on the face and breast, and thick as fur could grow. The wind drove the snow onto the windows with such force that it rattled like sleet, and the house trembled a little. Then all at once the Cat heard a noise, and stopped gnawing his rabbit and listened, his shining green eyes fixed upon a window. Then he heard a hoarse shout, a halloo of despair and entreaty; but he knew that it was not his master come home, and he waited, one paw still on the rabbit. Then the halloo came again, and then the Cat answered. He said all that was essential quite plainly to his own comprehension. There was in his cry of response inquiry, information, warning, terror, and finally, the offer of comradeship; but the man outside did not hear him, because of the great howling of the storm.

Then there was a great battering pound at the door, then another, and another. The Cat dragged his rabbit under the bed. The blows came thicker and faster. It was a weak arm which gave them, but it was nerved by desperation. Finally the lock yielded, and the stranger came in. Then the Cat peering from under the bed, blinked with a sudden light, and his green eyes narrowed. The stranger struck a match and looked about. The Cat saw a face wild and blue with hunger and cold, and a man who looked poorer and older than his poor old master, who was an outcast among men for his poverty and lowly mystery of antecedents; and he heard a muttered, unintelligible voicing of distress from the harsh, piteous mouth. There was in it both profanity and prayer, but the cat knew nothing of that.

The stranger braced the door which he had forced, got some wood from the stock in the corner, and kindled a fire in the old stove as quickly as his half-frozen hands would allow. He shook so pitiably as he worked that the Cat under the bed felt the tremor of it. Then the man, who was small and feeble and marked with the scars of suffering which he had pulled down upon his head, sat down in one of the old chairs and crouched over the fire as if it were the one love and desire of his soul, holding out his yellow hands

"...white on the face and breast, and thick as fur could grow."

like yellow claws, and he groaned. The Cat came out from under the bed and leapt upon his lap with the rabbit. The man gave a great shout and start of terror, and sprang, and the Cat slid clawing to the floor, and the rabbit fell inertly, and the man leaned, gasping with fright, and ghastly, against the wall. The Cat grabbed the rabbit by the slack of its neck and dragged it to the man's feet. Then he raised his shrill, insistent cry, he arched his back high, his tail was a splendid waving plume. He rubbed against the man's feet, which were bursting out of their torn shoes.

The man pushed the Cat away, gently enough, and began searching about the little cabin. He even climbed painfully the ladder to the loft and lit a match, and peered up in the darkness with straining eyes. He feared lest there might be a man, since there was a cat. His experience with men had not been pleasant, and neither had the experience of men been pleasant with him. He was an old wandering Ishmael among his kind; he had stumbled upon the house of a brother, and the brother was not home, and he was glad.

He returned to the Cat, and stooped stiffly and stroked his back, which the animal arched like the spring of a bow.

Then he took up the rabbit and looked at it eagerly by the firelight. His jaws worked. He could almost have devoured it raw. He fumbled – the Cat close at his heels – around some rude shelves and a table, and found with a grunt of self-gratulation, a lamp with oil in it. That he lighted; then he found a frying-pan and a knife, and skinned the rabbit, and prepared it for cooking, the Cat always at his feet.

When the odour of the cooking flesh filled the cabin, both the man and the Cat looked wolfish. The man turned the rabbit with one hand, and stooped to pat the Cat with the other. The Cat thought him a fine man. He loved him with all his heart, though he had known him such a short time, and though the man had a face both pitiful and sharply set at variance with the best of things.

It was a face with the grimy grizzle of age upon it, with fever hollows in the cheeks, and the memories of wrong in the dim eyes, but the Cat accepted the man unquestioningly and loved him. When the rabbit was half cooked neither the man nor the Cat could wait any longer. The man took it from the fire, divided it exactly in halves, gave the Cat one, and took the other himself. Then they ate.

Then the man blew out the light, called the cat to him, got on the bed, drew up the ragged coverings, and fell asleep with the Cat on his bosom.

The man was the Cat's guest all the rest of the winter, and the winter is long in the mountains. The rightful owner of the little hut did not return until May. All that time the Cat toiled hard, and he grew rather thin himself, for he shared everything except mice with his guest; and sometimes game was wary, and the fruit of the patience of days was very little for two. The man was ill and weak, however, and unable to eat much, which was fortunate, since he could not hunt for himself. All day long he lay on the bed, or else sat crouched over the fire. It was a good thing that firewood was ready at hand for picking up, not a stone's throw from the door, for that he had to attend to himself.

The Cat foraged tirelessly. Sometimes he was gone for days together, and at first the man used to be terrified, thinking that he would never return; then he would hear the familiar cry at the door, and stumble to his feet and let him in. Then the two would dine together, sharing equally; then the Cat would rest and purr, and finally sleep in the man's arms.

Towards spring the game grew more plentiful; more wild little quarry were tempted out of their homes, in search of love as well as food. One day the Cat had luck – a rabbit, a partridge and a mouse. He could not carry them all at once, but finally he had them together at the house door. Then he cried but no one answered. All the mountain streams were loosened and the air was full of the gurgle of many waters, occasionally pierced by a bird whistle. The trees rustled with a new sound to the spring wind; there was a flush of rose and gold-green on the breasting surface of a distant mountain seen through an opening in the wood. The tips of the bushes were swollen and glistening red, and now and then there was a flower; but the Cat had nothing to do with flowers. He stood beside his booty at the house door, and cried and cried with his insistent triumph and complaint and pleading, but no one came to let him in. Then the Cat left his treasures at the door, and went around to the back of the house to the pine-tree, and was up the trunk with a wild scramble, and in through his little window, and down through the trap to the room, and the man was gone.

The Cat cried again – that cry of the animal for human companionship, which is one of the sad notes of the world; he looked in all the corners; he sprang to the chair at the window and looked out; but no one came. The man was gone, and he never came again.

The Cat ate his mouse on the turf beside the house; the rabbit and the partridge he carried painfully into the house, but the man did not come to share them. Finally, in the course of a day or two, he ate them up himself; then he slept a long time on the bed, and when he waked the man was not there.

Then the Cat went forth to his hunting-grounds again, and came home at night with a plump bird, reasoning with his tireless persistency in expectancy that the man would be there; and there was a light in the window, and when he cried his old master opened the door and let him in.

His master had a strong comradeship with the Cat, but not affection. He never patted him like that gentler outcast, but he had a pride in him, and an anxiety for his welfare, though he had left him alone all winter without scruple. He feared lest some misfortune might have come to the Cat, though he was so large of his kind, and a mighty hunter. Therefore, when he saw him in the door in all the glory of his winter coat, his white breast and face shining like snow in the sun, his own face lit up with welcome, and the Cat embraced his feet with his sinuous body vibrant with rejoicing purrs.

The Cat had the bird to himself, for his master had his own supper already cooking on the stove. After supper the Cat's master took his pipe, and sought a small store of tobacco which he had left in his hut over winter. He had thought often of it; that and the Cat seemed something to come home to in the spring. But the tobacco had gone; not a dust left. The man swore in a grim little monotone, which made the profanity lose its customary effect. He had been, and was, a hard drinker; he had knocked about the world until the marks of its sharp corners were on his very soul, which was thereby calloused, until his very sensibility to loss was dulled. He was a very old man.

He searched for the tobacco with a sort of dull combativeness of persistency; then he stared with stupid wonder around the room. Suddenly many features struck him as being changed. Another stove-lid was broken; an old piece of carpet was tacked up over a window to keep out the cold; his fire-wood was gone. He looked, and there was no oil left in his can. He looked at the coverings on his bed; he took them up, and again made that strange remonstrant noise in his throat. Then he looked again for his tobacco.

Finally he gave it up. He sat down beside the fire, for May in the mountains is cold; he held up his empty pipe in his mouth, his rough forehead knitted, and he and the Cat looked at each other across that impassable barrier of silence which has been set between man and beast from the creation of the world.

"...one up a tree
one under the tree..."

Diamond Cut Diamond

EWART MILNE

Two cats

One up a tree

One under the tree

The Cat up a tree is he

The cat under a tree is she

The tree is witch elm, just incidentally.

He takes no notice of she, she takes no notice of he.

He stares at the woolly clouds passing, she stares at the tree.

There's been a lot written about cats, by Old Possum, Yeats and Company

But not Alfred de Musset or Lord Tennyson or Poe or anybody

Wrote about one cat under, and one cat up, a tree.

God knows why this should be left for me

Except I like cats as cats be

Especially one cat up

And one under

A witch elm

Tree

The Cat Horoscope

MICHAELA FRIEDERIKE

"A dreamer..."

SAGITTARIUS (November 23 - December 21)

A dreamer who's not really in touch with reality. Can appear scatterbrained but is really intelligent and always willing to please. The diplomat of the cat-world; not argumentative or difficult but although accomodating he can sometimes be surprisingly clumsy. Sagittarians are usually either big and strong or smaller than average, but with a robust little figure!

Best Owners: Other Sagittarians (they suit each other...).
Famous Sagittarians: Beethoven, Wm. Blake, Churchill, Jimi Hendrix, Billy the Kid, Toulouse Lautrec, Nostradamus, Edith Piaf, Mark Twain.

Thoughts and Doubts

RAY FLINT

I think it's true that kittenhood
Was quite the best time of my life
When first I learnt what claws were for
And how to push an open door:
That little mews would gain me all
From catnip fish to woollen ball.
I soon had learned the sound of knife
On plate or tin that meant my food.
Such bliss!
But then when I grew into Cat
And took my place before the fire
I heard them (not quite seriously) say
I should not dream my days away
And I should learn a trade and be
A model of self-sufficiency.
This was the time to slink, retire
To ponder what they meant by that.
And think.

I could not live a life at sea
With horrid rats and scaly fish
I'ld miss too much the trees and birds
And my pet humans' gentle words.
I wonder if a farm would do
And I might learn to plough and sow
But that's a very foolish wish,
With my small paws it could not be.
Grow up!
I do not know Dick Whittington
And if I did the place is filled
And I wouldn't want to fight
Because I try to do what's right
So what is left? Perhaps a stable
Full of mice but I'm unable
To contemplate the mice I've killed:
Purrs would not mean absolution.
I'm a coward.
Perhaps when overhearing chat
They talked of someone else and that
They wouldn't mind if here I stayed
Guarded by the saw toothed blade
To watch the crab whilst horse and sheep
Patrol the wall where dancers leap
And keep my whiskers delicate.
Perhaps I'll stay a Carpet Cat.
Much better!

"Perhaps I'll stay a Carpet Cat."

The Cat

GILES LYTTON-STRACHEY

"With tail erect and pompous march…"

Dear creature by the fire a-purr,
Strange idol, eminently bland,
Miraculous puss! As o'er your fur
I trail a negligible hand

And gaze into your gazing eyes,
And wonder in a demi-dream
What mystery it is that lies
Behind those slits that glare and gleam,

An exquisite enchantment falls
About the portals of my sense;
Meandering through the enormous halls
I breathe luxurious frankincense.

An ampler air, a warmer June
Enfold me, and my wandering eye
Salutes a more imperial moon
Throned in a more resplendent sky

Than ever knew this northern shore.
Oh, strange! For you are with me too,
And I, who am a cat once more,
Follow the woman that was you.

With tail erect and pompous march,
The proudest puss that ever trod,
Through many a grove, 'neath many an arch,
Impenetrable as a god,

Down many an alabaster flight
Of broad and cedar-shaded stairs,
Whilst over us the elaborate night
Mysteriously gleams and glares!

The Tyger

WM BLAKE

"What immortal hand or eye
Could frame thy fearful symmetry?"

Tyger! Tyger! Burning bright
In the forests of the night,
What immortal hand or eye
Could frame thy fearful symmetry?

In what distant deeps or skies
Burnt the fire of thine eyes?
On what wings dare he aspire?
What the hand dare seize the fire?

And what shoulder, and what art,
Could twist the sinews of thy heart?
And when thy heart began to beat,
What dread hand? And what dread feet?

What the hammer? What the chain?
In what furnace was thy brain?
What the anvil? What dread grasp
Dare its deadly terror clasp?
When the stars threw down their spears,
And water'd heaven with their tears,
Did he smile his work to see?
Did he who made the Lamb make thee?

Tyger! Tyger! Burning bright
In the forests of the night,
What immortal hand or eye
Could frame thy fearful symmetry?

Complacent Cat

MARY MORROW LINDBERGH

"...so self-satisfied, so complacent."

I saw the most beautiful cat today. It was sitting by the side of the road, its two front feet neatly and graciously together. Then it gravely swished around its tail to completely and snugly encircle itself. It was so fit and beautifully neat, that gesture, and so self-satisfied, so complacent.

Cat-Goddesses

ROBERT GRAVES

"...the blackest of them..."

A perverse habit of cat-goddesses –
Even the blackest of them, black as coals
Save for a new moon blazing on each breast,
With coral tongues and beryl eyes like lamps,
Long-leggèd, pacing three by three in nines –
This obstinate habit is to yield themselves
In verisimilar love-ecstasies,
To tatter-eared and slinking alley-toms
No less below the common run of cats
Than they above it; which they do for spite,
To provoke jealousy – and not the least abashed
By such gross-headed, rabbit-coloured litters
As soon they shall be happy to desert.

Growling

PETER GRAY

A mother cat warns her kittens of danger by growling at them and the kittens know what she means. A mother warns off another cat or dog by growling and the kittens know what she means. A mother cat warns the kittens off her own food by growling and they know what she means. These growls sound all the same to humans but not, evidently, to cats.

"...the kittens know what she means."

Tabbies

DITZ

There was a fat tabby called Bunny,
Who loved cuddling up with his honey,
(a whippet, called Tabby
who'd never get flabby),
On cushions in places quite sunny.

"...cuddling up with his honey"

The Cat Horoscope

MICHAELA FRIEDERIKE

"This is a serious cat..."

CAPRICORN (December 22 - January 20)

This is a serious, complex, intelligent and calculating cat. Generally not very relaxed, he doesn't make friends easily, tends to lead a solitary life and doesn't like to be the centre of attention.

Best Owners: Virgo (the choosy perfectionist can accept the sometimes aloof nature of the Capricorn cat).
Famous Capricorns: Joan Baez, Marlene Dietrich, Joan of Arc, Martin Luther King, Kipling, Matisse, Dolly Parton, Elvis Presley, JRR Tolkien.

Mother

JOHN KEATS

"...the Mother is a tabby..."

Mrs Dilke has two cats – a Mother and a Daughter – now the Mother is a tabby and the daughter a black and white like the spotted child – now it appears ominous to me for the doors of both houses are opened frequently – so there is a complete thoroughfare for both Cats (there being no board up to the contrary) they may one and several of them come into my room ad libitum... But no – the Tabby only comes – whether from sympathy from Ann the maid or me I can not tell – or whether Brown has left behind him any atmosphere spirit of Maidenhood I can not tell. The Cat is not an old Maid herself – her daughter is a proof of it – I have questioned her – I have look'd at the lines of her paws – I have felt her pulse – to no purpose – why should the old Cat come to me? I ask myself – and myself has not a word to answer.

Cats

ELEANOR FARJEON

Cats sleep
Anywhere,
Any table,
Any chair,
Top of piano,
Window-ledge,
In the middle,
On the edge,
Open drawer,
Empty shoe,
Anybody's
Lap will do,
Fitted in a
Cardboard box,
In the cupboard
With your frocks –
Anywhere!
They don't care!
Cats sleep
Anywhere.

"…window-ledge…"

From

Bluebell: Diary of a Cat Branching Out

JAN D'LORD

8th July

All right, I admit it! I was stuck up a tree. But I wasn't the only one, that Jenny was waving around in the breeze just beneath me.

She said she had come up to rescue me, but don't believe a word of it, she can't let me have any peace or enjoyment.

It was a bit of a surprise when I ran after a fluffy-tailed squirrel which jumped to another tree when it reached the top. It disappeared from view but there was nowhere for me to go. The ground was an awfully long way down. Jenny said she heard my desperate miaowing from the kitchen where she was toasting crumpets. I was actually singing, the view was worth praising in my melodic voice. I could see over a church, the top of our garage and next door's washing. Did you know he wears long, fleecy underwear?

I would have come down at my own pace when I'd had enough spying on the neighbours, but no, Jenny came panting up behind me gasping for breath and calling, "Booby-doos, don't worry, mummy is here."

Well I wasn't worried until she arrived clinging and wobbling, with leaves stuck in her hair and scratches all over her arms. She was clutching at me and spoiling everything, so I jumped onto the fence and then behind the lilac.

"All right, I admit it! I was stuck up a tree."

Jenny didn't come down. In fact she stayed up there for two hours. I licked the butter from the crumpets, knocked them to the floor for the puppies and then stuck my paw into the strawberry jam. It was great. I had a sleep on the new sofa and only woke when she started singing about the view herself, only she didn't seem to like it, she was trilling, "Oh, it's so awful up here. Somebody…anybody, help!"

I went outside and had a look. Her bottom doesn't half look big in those jeans and with her legs wrapped around a tree trunk. I don't know why she stayed up so long, it was getting dark. Headlights filled the drive and Ross was home. I ran to him for a cuddle. It was a good, ear-rubbing one, so when Jenny started on with that song again, I purred extra loud so that he couldn't hear. Ross switched on the kitchen lights and I gave him the where's-my-dinner-then rub.

"Sorry Bluebell, don't know where the tin opener has got to. You'll have to wait till Jenny comes in. Where on earth has she gone, leaving the place in such a mess?"

No dinner! I had little choice, I ran to the door so he'd let me out into the back garden. He heard the screaming then. She soon ran out of songs.

It was great. He got out a ladder and I went up the tree again, the easy way. I had to get down quickly this time or he would have stood on my paws.

Jenny spent what was left of the evening on the sofa. So I sat on her tummy going up and down with the snores. She was too upset to think of the tin opener so Ross and I had fish and chips whilst he praised me for showing him where Jenny was.

She takes some looking after I can tell you. After that she learnt to use a ladder but we both stayed away from trees for quite a while. I didn't think the kittens would dare to climb up something so big when they were so little but they would have to learn eventually. As usual, I would give them the benefit of my considerable experience.

The chance came sooner than I expected.

I was on Jenny's knee as she was ordering a take-away. She was telling the man how to get to Ha'penny Hollow with his 'Flying Pizza', whatever that is.

"Turn left at that bush with all the pink blossom, bend with the road where the lovely white pussy cat always sits and you know when you reach that house with the door newly painted in heavenly blue…turn right. We are the house with more lavender bushes than next door."

"Can I speak to someone more sensible please?" the exasperated voice filled mine and Jenny's ears.

"Cheek!" she said handing Ross the phone.

He spoke in a voice as close to that of a sensible person as he possibly could. He guided the delivery man by pubs. They were both happy with that.

I hung around hoping for a lick of pizza crust but it had chili on.

My first brush with chili was also my last. I had one tongue touch and ran at a million miles an hour out of the flap and up a tree without even thinking. I was there for ages. Jenny said it served me right for pinching human's food so she wouldn't come with any help.

That was winter and I was very cold. I thought of that branch now and how high it was. I wondered why my weight hadn't brought the tree down or at least the branch - the higher you get the thinner the branches.

I didn't want to risk it again but I remembered everything about the journey and the climb. It took only seconds, yet I was so scared every little thing stuck clearly in my mind. The kittens ambled in, drawn by the smell. I told them not to bother, they'd end up on thin twigs. But they were bored.

I asked them if they wanted to have the best view of a lovely summer's evening that was possible. Farthing and Dandelion suddenly went wide-eyed with wonder. There weren't many places they hadn't explored around here. Something new was exciting.

I didn't want to go up there again so I told them the way. We had perfected our mental communication and with the help of a few chirrups and a couple of nose points they were off.

I knew they would be going through my directions in their little heads.

"Past the black plastic bin that always smells of fish, up the winding path which pushes gravel between your toes, around the bush where that horrible tom cat sprays every night and on to the wall where we watch the hedgehog hunting slugs. Across to where we lay on the bluebells, right on to where we squashed the forget-me-nots. Stop at the mousehole where we always stick our paws in right up to our shoulders but never find anything. Just behind is a fat tree with bark where those busy ants live. Start climbing just beside the ivy leaves where we pounce on sunbathing bees."

I knew they'd be there together and could see in my minds eye as they continued past a branch that looked like Jenny's arms when she was throwing them about in a cross mood. I'd directed them to a higher branch which had leaves sticking out all over like Ross's hair on a windy day.

I went to sleep then and forgot about them.

When I woke it was dark and Jenny was prodding me with an urgent finger.

"Bluebell! We haven't seen the kittens for hours and they haven't come in for supper. Do you know where they are?"

My first reaction was to rush to the food bowl and scoff the lot. Jenny wasn't letting me off the cushion until I helped. I was keen because she stood in the way of that chopped-up liver, the smell of which was wafting round the house. I wasn't going out, so I would have to try to get through that thick skull of hers. I went through the directions again mentally, very quickly. Do you know, she didn't even thank me!

"Oh Bluebell, you are no use! I suppose I'll have to find them myself."

She went out then and I jumped onto the windowsill. Amazingly, she followed the exact route those kittens had taken!

As I ate, I saw her stout shoes and the bottom of a ladder pass the cat-flap. Minutes later Farthing and Dandelion had joined the rest of us cats at the four bowls.

I should have told Ross, then I'd have had more liver. He would never have understood. There are no pubs on the way to the walnut tree.

"…beside the ivy leaves…"

"She sights a Bird – she chuckles…"

She Sights A Bird

EMILY DICKINSON

She sights a Bird – she chuckles –
She flattens – then she crawls –
She runs without the look of feet –
Her eyes increase to Balls –

Her Jaws stir – twitching – hungry –
Her Teeth can hardly stand –

She leaps, but Robin leaped the first –
Ah, Pussy, of the Sand,

The Hopes so juicy ripening –
You almost bathed your Tongue –
When Bliss disclosed a hundred Toes –
And fled with every one -

Theodore Roosevelt's Cats

THEODORE ROOSEVELT

White House, 6th January, 1903

Dear Kermit,

We felt very melancholy after you and Ted left and the house seemed empty and lonely. But it was the greatest possible comfort to feel that you both really have enjoyed school and are both doing well there.

Tom Quartz is certainly the cunningest kitten I have ever seen. He is always playing pranks on Jack and I get very nervous lest Jack should grow too irritated. The other evening they were both in the library – Jack sleeping before the fire – Tom Quartz scampering about, an exceedingly playful little creature – which is about what he is. He would race across the floor, then jump upon the curtain or play with the tassel. Suddenly he spied Jack and galloped up to him. Jack, looking exceedingly sullen and shame-faced, jumped out of the way and got upon the sofa and around the table, and Tom Quartz instantly jumped on him again. Jack suddenly shifted to the other sofa, where Tom Quartz again went after him. Then Jack started for the door, while Tom made a rapid turn under the sofa and around the table and just as Jack reached the door leapt on his hindquarters. Jack bounded forward and away the two went tandem out of the room – Jack not co-operating at all; and about five minutes afterwards Tom Quartz stalked solemnly back.

"...the cunningest kitten I have ever seen."

Another evening, the next Speaker of the House, Mr Cannon, an exceedingly solemn, elderly gentleman with chin whiskers, who does certainly not look to be of playful nature, came to call upon me. He is a great friend of mine, and we sat talking over what our policies for the session should be until about eleven o'clock and when he went away I accompanied him to the head of the stairs. He had gone about half-way down when Tom Quartz strolled by, his tail erect and very fluffy. He spied Mr Cannon going down the stairs, jumped to the conclusion that he was a playmate escaping, and raced after him, suddenly grasping him by the leg the way he does Archie and Quentin when they play hide and seek with him; then loosening his hold he tore downstairs ahead of Mr Cannon, who eyed him with an iron calm and not one particle of surprise…

The Cat Horoscope

MICHAELA FRIEDERIKE

"…loves to play…"

AQUARIUS (January 21 - February 19)

Expect the unexpected! This cat is trouble but always fun. Loves people, loves to play, even loves dogs, but can be changeable and spread his affections widely. Don't expect him to stay on your lap if someone more interesting walks into the room…

Best Owners: Libra (calm, introverted, Librans and Aquarians are no competition for each other…), other Aquarians can also be good.
Famous Aquarians: Lewis Carroll, Charles Darwin, James Dean, Charles Dickens, Abraham Lincoln, Bob Marley, Mozart, FD Roosevelt, Schubert.

C

EDWARD LEAR

"…its eyes were large and pale…"

C was a lovely Pussy Cat; its eyes were large and pale;

And on its back he had some stripes,

And several on his tail.

From

The Retired Cat

WILLIAM COWPER

A drawer, it chanced, at bottom lined
With linen of the softest kind,
With such as merchants introduce
From India, for ladies' use,
A drawer impending o'er the rest,
Half open in the topmost chest,
Of depth enough, and none to spare,
Invited her to slumber there;
Puss with delight beyond expression
Surveyed the scene, and took possession.
Recumbent at her ease, ere long,
And lulled by her own humdrum song,
She left the cares of life behind,
And slept as she would sleep her last,
When in came, housewifely inclined,
The chambermaid, and shut it fast;
By no malignity impelled,
But all unconscious whom it held.
Awakened by the shock (cried Puss)
"Was ever cat attended thus?
The open drawer was left, I see,

Merely to provide a nest for me,
For soon as I was well composed,
Then came the maid, and it was closed.
How smooth these 'kerchiefs, and how sweet!
Oh what a delicate retreat!
I will resign myself to rest
Till Sol, declining in the West,
Shall call to supper, when, no doubt
Susan will come and let me out."
The evening came, the sun descended,
And Puss remained still unattended.
The night rolled tardily away,
(With her indeed, t'was never day,)
The sprightly morn her course renewed,
The evening gray again ensued,
And Puss came into mind no more
Than if entombed the day before.
With hunger pinched, and pinched for room,
She now presaged approaching doom
Nor slept a single wink or purred,
Conscious of jeopardy incurred.
That night, by chance, the poet watching,
Heard an inexplicable scratching;
His noble heart went pit-a-pat,
And to himself he said – "What's that?"
He drew the curtain at his side,
And forth he peeped, but nothing spied.

Yet, by his ear directed, guessed
Something imprisoned in the chest,
And, doubtful what, with prudent care
Resolved it should continue there.
At length a voice which well he knew,
A long and melancholy mew,
Saluting his poetic ears,
Consoled him and dispelled his fears:
He left his bed, he trod the floor,
He 'gan in haste the drawers to explore,
The lowest first, and without stop
The rest in order to the top.
For 'tis a truth well known to most
That whatsoever thing is lost,
We seek it, ere it come to light,
In every cranny but the right.
Forth skipped the cat, not now replete
As erst with airy self-conceit,
Nor in her own fond apprehension
A theme for all the world's attention
But modest, sober, cured of all
Her notions hyperbolical,
And wishing for a place of rest
Anything rather than a chest.

"Forth skipped the cat..."

From

A Clergyman's Daughter

GEORGE ORWELL

Dorothy knocked at the Pithers' badly-fitting door, from beneath which a melancholy smell of boiled cabbage and dishwater was oozing. From long experience she knew and could taste in advance the individual smell of every cottage on her rounds. Some of the smells were peculiar in the extreme. For instance, there was the salty, feral smell that haunted the cottage of old Mr. Tombs, an aged retired bookseller who lay in bed all day in a darkened room, with his long, dusty nose and pebble spectacles protruding from what appeared to be a fur rug of vast size and richness. But if you put your hand on the fur rug it disintegrated, burst and fled in all directions. It was composed entirely of cats - twenty-four cats, to be exact. Mr. Tombs "found they kept him warm", he used to explain.

"..the fur rug was composed entirely of cats…"

"...pussy and I very gently will play."

I Love Little Pussy

ANON

I love little pussy, her coat is so warm;
And if I don't hurt her she'll do me no harm.
So I'll not pull her tail, nor drive her away,
But pussy and I very gently will play.
She shall sit by my side and I'll give her some food;
And she'll love me because I am gentle and good.

I'll pat pretty pussy, and then she will purr;
And thus show her thanks for my kindness to her.
But I'll not pinch her ears, nor tread on her paw,
Lest I should provoke her to use her sharp claw.
I never will vex her, nor make her displeased,
For pussy don't like to be worried and teased.

Dresser Cats

SYLVIA TOWNSEND WARNER

"…two cats on a dresser…"

I wish you could see the two cats side by side on a Victorian dresser, their paws, their ears, their tails complementally adjusted, their blue eyes blinking open on a single thought of when I shall remember it's their suppertime. They might have been composed by Bach for two flutes.

The Cat Horoscope

MICHAELA FRIEDERIKE

"...often withdrawn and unapproachable."

PISCES (February 20 - March 20)

Moody, changeable, a play-actor. Sometimes friendly but often withdrawn and unapproachable. There will be occasions when you think he's deliberately trying to be awkward but swimming against the tide is what Pisceans do best! Going with the flow is too easy...

Best Owners: Cancer or Scorpio (both strong, independent grown-up types...).
Famous Pisceans: Caruso, Chopin, Einstein, George Harrison, Victor Hugo, Michelangelo, Nureyev, Renoir, Elizabeth Taylor, George Washington.

Verses on a Cat

PERCY BYSSHE SHELLEY

"But this poor little cat only wanted a rat..."

A cat in distress,
Nothing more, nor less
Good folks, I must faithfully tell ye,
As I am a sinner,
It waits for some dinner,
To stuff out its own little belly.

You would not easily guess
All the modes of distress
Which torture the tenants of earth;
And the various evils,
Which, like so many devils,
Attend the poor souls from their birth.

Some living require,
And others desire
An old fellow out of the way;
And which is best
I leave to be guessed,
For I cannot pretend to say.

One wants society,
Another variety,
Others a tranquil life;
Some want food,
Others, as good,
Only want a wife.

But this poor little cat
Only wanted a rat,
To stuff out its own little maw;
And it were as good
Some people had such food,
To make them hold their jaw!

Geraniums

ERNEST H SHEPHARD

"...pots of geraniums on the high windowsill..."

There were pots of geraniums on the high windowsill, with a tortoiseshell cat curled up between them where the sun made a splash. Cyril went across and stroked it - he was always fond of cats - and it got up, stretched itself, arched its back and purred. The clock ticked on slowly, and there was a faint buzzing of bees. It seemed as if nothing wanted to wake up.

A Modest Cat's Soliloquy

ANON

"...my morning nap."

Far down within the damp dark earth
The grimy miner goes
That I on chilly nights may have
A fire to warm my toes;
Brave sailors plow the wintry main
Through peril and mishap,
That I, on Oriental rugs
May take my morning nap.
Out in the distant meadow
Meekly gaze the lowing kine,
That milk in endless saucerfulls,
All foaming, may be mine;
The fish that swim the ocean
And the birds that fill the air,
Did I not like to pick their bones,
Pray, think you, they'd be there?

From

The Tragic Sense of Life

MIGUEL DE UNAMUNO

What differentiates man
from other animals
is perhaps feeling
rather than reason.
I have seen a cat
reason more often
than laugh or weep.
Perhaps it laughs or weeps
within itself…

"I have seen a cat reason..."

The Mistress of the Cats

Ditz was born in Vienna, Austria but has lived in England for over 30 years. Her distinctive style has evolved over time into the highly detailed, quirky images that will be easily recognized from books, greetings cards, jigsaw puzzles, stationery products, ceramics and textiles. The paintings themselves, usually on a relatively small scale, are in acrylic on board and her favourite (though not sole) subjects are cats... Ditz has exhibited regularly at a range of galleries including The Royal Academy (many times) and The Barbican (both London), also in civic museums and galleries in other UK and European cities. Her work hangs in collections throughout the world.

To see more of her work or to buy prints
or original paintings visit her website at
www.aappl.com or write to her c/o info@aappl.com

Acknowledgements

The Publisher has made every effort to contact the Copyright holders and offers apologies to any he has been unable to trace or for any incorrect information. Grateful acknowledgement is made for permission to reproduce the following:

	page
CAT (from *Brownjohn's Beasts*) by Alan Brownjohn: Macmillan Publishers, London	70
MY BOSS THE CAT by Paul Gallico: Gillon Aitken Associates Ltd., copyright © Mathemata AG 1964	72
A CAT by Julie Brown: permission of AAPPL	81
WAVE-SILK TABBY by Joy Flint: permission of AAPPL	83
THE STORY OF WEBSTER (from *The World of Mr Mulliner*) by PG Wodehouse: published by Barrie & Jenkins, by permission of The Random House Group Ltd and AP Watt on behalf of the trustees of the Wodehouse Estate	88
WHY? by Christopher Guy: permission of AAPPL	118
TERRY (from *A Fourth Poetry Book*) by Albert Rowe: Oxford University Press	122
COUNTRY CAT (from *Night and the Cat*) by Elizabeth Coatsworth: Macmillan Publishers, London and Simon & Schuster, NY	138
THOUGHTS AND DOUBTS by Ray Flint: permission of AAPPL	177
CAT GODDESSES (from *Complete Poems*) by Robert Graves: permission of Carcanet Press Ltd	185
TABBIES by Ditz: permission of AAPPL	187
CATS (from *Blackbird has Spoken*, published by Macmillan) by Eleanor Farjeon: permission of David Higham Associates Ltd	190
BLUEBELL (from *Bluebell – Diary of a Cat Branching Out*) by Jan D'Lord: permission of Michael O'Mara Books	192
THE CAT HOROSCOPE by Michaela Friederike: permission of AAPPL	various